"It is no secret that people worldwide are increasingly disconnected from each other. For a number of reasons, we are detached from feeling we can be vulnerable about ourselves with others. This issue ties directly into massive problems in physical, emotional, relational, and spiritual health. Todd Hall has provided a biblical and scientifically validated path to learn and experience true connection with God, others, and our very selves. The chapters on relational knowledge are a highlight. I highly recommend this book."

John Townsend, author of the Boundaries book series and founder of the Townsend Institute for Leadership and Counseling

"People seem more relationally disconnected today than ever and yet are desperate for meaning and connection. This is one big reason I am thrilled about this new book by my friend Todd Hall. *The Connected Life* is research based and yet full of stories and practical ideas. I am honored to offer an endorsement and look forward to helping spread the word when it releases."

Sean McDowell, professor at Biola University and author of *So the Next Generation Will Know*

"We live in the most distracted and disrupted culture in the history of the world. That radical disruption is affecting our families, personal relationships, careers, and spiritual lives, which is why I'm so thrilled Todd Hall has released *The Connected Life*. The truth is, this book is a road map for navigating today's world—if you can't change, the world will pass you by. So read *The Connected Life*, underline it, and keep it on your desk. It could very well be your ticket to the future."

Phil Cooke, filmmaker and media consultant, author of *One Big Thing: Discovering What You Were Born to Do*

"*The Connected Life* is a brilliant book that is very important for the future of the church. It offers practical insights that will help you find meaning and thrive in life. Drawn from Todd's faith, personal experiences, counseling practice, and psychology research, *The Connected Life* brings a fresh perspective. Todd's beautiful writing style really connects, and his storytelling ability is icing on the cake."

Michael Lee Stallard, president of Connection Culture Group and author of *Connection Culture: The Competitive Advantage of Shared Identity, Empathy, and Understanding at Work*

"Although most of us recognize the importance of relationships in our lives at some level, we often find ourselves stuck, unsure of how to cultivate healthy, thriving relationships. In this book, Todd clarifies the path toward adopting new habits and frameworks that help us to love others and ourselves well. *The Connected Life* communicates profound insights about how to love winsomely and live meaningfully."

Steve Saccone, author of *Relational Intelligence* and *Talking About God*

"*The Connected Life* blends social science with spiritual truths to reveal why we feel so discombobulated, and tells us how to put ourselves back together."

David Burkus, author of *The Myths of Creativity* and *Friend of a Friend*

"In *The Connected Life*, Todd Hall demonstrates powerfully that we are hardwired for close, empathic relationships, but we suffer deeply from our increasingly fragmented culture. Through compelling stories, research results clearly explained, and practical action steps, Todd helps readers learn how to build life-giving relational connections. This book challenged me and fed my soul. I heartily recommend it."

Joshua Miller, author of *Unrepeatable: Cultivating the Unique Calling of Every Person*

"Todd Hall understands the connected life, largely because he's known firsthand the disconnected life. He grew up looking for love, longing for a place to belong. Thankfully, he found it all, and more, in the welcome of a good God, the love of a good woman, and the grace of a good church. But he knows deeply and clearly what it is to lack such things, so he also knows the gifts that these things are and how best to receive, foster, and steward them. How do you or I overcome our tendencies to hide, evade, resist, and resent? How do we truly, deeply connect? I can hardly think of a question more relevant to our times or one for which we need, and urgently, real wisdom. This book is just such wisdom."

Mark Buchanan, pastor and author of *Spiritual Rhythm*

"I love that the thoughtful engagement with neuroscience, attachment psychology, theology, and more from Todd's previous book is now offered in this engaging and accessible work. *The Connected Life* offers a kind of antidote to our disconnected lives and to the hidden suffering we endure as a result. It envisions a way back to each other and to God."

Chuck DeGroat, professor of pastoral care and Christian spirituality at Western Theological Seminary

"We live in a world where 'friends' usually means contacts, accountability most often refers to associates, and the best intimacy means FaceTime. Todd Hall challenges us to examine our earthly relationships in light of the potential and power of the spiritual glue that can hold them together. *The Connected Life* presents an oasis of hope in a desert of disconnection."

Kenneth C. Ulmer, senior advisor to the president, Biola University

"Todd Hall has written a very helpful and relevant book for our fragmented and broken world, focusing on relational spirituality and the connected life we all deeply long for and that can be found in the love of God in Christ and in the loving community of the church. Highly recommended as essential reading for all of us!"

Siang-Yang Tan, senior professor of clinical psychology at Fuller Theological Seminary and author of *Counseling and Psychotherapy: A Christian Perspective*

"By weaving personal stories with psychological theory and research, Dr. Hall guides his readers to an understanding of healthy attachment and the way in which it can heal. His soulful explanation of psychological theory provides a guidebook of sorts for how we can be more deeply connected to ourselves, each other, and God. This book will help readers understand themselves—and those they care for—better and more deeply, enhancing their relationships and creating the conditions for better health and transformed connections."

Doreen Dodgen-Magee, psychologist and author of *Restart: Designing a Healthy Post-Pandemic Life*

"Todd Hall has spent his career plumbing the practical aspects of psychology and drawing out the deep connections with Christian theology. In *The Connected Life*, he marshals all his wisdom to help us understand the best way to live, love, and lead. This book will provide more practical *aha!* moments than any book you'll read this year. I highly recommend it!"

Ken Wytsma, author of *The Grand Paradox* and *The Myth of Equality*

TODD W. HALL

Foreword by CURT THOMPSON

The
Connected
Life

The ART and SCIENCE of
RELATIONAL SPIRITUALITY

An imprint of InterVarsity Press
Downers Grove, Illinois

InterVarsity Press
P.O. Box 1400, Downers Grove, IL 60515-1426
ivpress.com
email@ivpress.com

InterVarsity Press® is a resource publishing division of InterVarsity Christian Fellowship/USA®. For information, visit intervarsity.org.

Unless otherwise indicated, all Scripture quotations are taken from the Holy Bible, New Living Translation, copyright ©1996, 2004, 2007, 2013. Used by permission of Tyndale House Publishers, Inc., Carol Stream, Illinois 60188. All rights reserved.

While any stories in this book are true, all names and identifying information have been changed, and in some cases elements from multiple clients have been combined, in order to protect the privacy of individuals.

Published in association with The Denzel Agency, www.denzelagency.com.

Portions of chapters 8, 11, 12, and 13 include content adapted from chapters 5 and 8 of Relational Spirituality *by Todd W. Hall with M. Elizabeth Lewis Hall. ©2021 by Todd W. Hall and Miriam Elizabeth Lewis Hall. Used by permission of InterVarsity Press, Downers Grove, IL.*

Cover design and image composite: David Fassett
Interior design: Daniel van Loon
Images: paper texture: 04 TGTS-Fibre-Board, True Grit Texture Supply
* geometric design pattern: 826735872, © Tomiganka / iStock / Getty Images Plus*

The publisher cannot verify the accuracy or functionality of website URLs used in this book beyond the date of publication.

ISBN 978-1-5140-0261-2 (print)
ISBN 978-1-5140-0262-9 (digital)

Printed in the United States of America ♾

InterVarsity Press is committed to ecological stewardship and to the conservation of natural resources in all our operations. This book was printed using sustainably sourced paper.

Library of Congress Cataloging-in-Publication Data
Names: Hall, Todd W., author.
Title: The connected life : the art and science of relational spirituality / Dr. Todd W. Hall.
Description: Downers Grove, IL : InterVarsity Press, [2022] | Includes bibliographical references.
Identifiers: LCCN 2022004059 (print) | LCCN 2022004060 (ebook) | ISBN 9781514002612 (hardcover) |
* ISBN 9781514002629 (ebook)*
Subjects: LCSH: Interpersonal relations—Religious aspects—Christianity. | Spiritual formation—Christianity.
Classification: LCC BV4597.52 .H345 2022 (print) | LCC BV4597.52 (ebook) | DDC 248.4—dc23/
* eng/20220301*
LC record available at https://lccn.loc.gov/2022004059
LC ebook record available at https://lccn.loc.gov/2022004060

P 21 20 19 18 17 16 15 14 13 12 11 10 9 8 7 6 5 4 3 2 1

Y 40 39 38 37 36 35 34 33 32 31 30 29 28 27 26 25 24 23 22

I dedicate this book to my wife, Liz,

who has selflessly helped me, in countless ways,

to grow toward living a connected life.

Contents

Foreword by Curt Thompson, MD *1*

Introduction: The Power of Loving Connection *3*

PART ONE: THE CONNECTION CRISIS

  1 The Causes of Our Connection Crisis *7*

  2 The Spiritual Effects of Our Connection Crisis *20*

  3 Misguided Spirituality *31*

PART TWO: RELATIONAL KNOWLEDGE

  4 We Know More Than We Can Say *43*

  5 Once More with Feeling *58*

PART THREE: ATTACHMENT BONDS

  6 Born to Connect *77*

  7 Becoming Attached *87*

  8 How We Connect to God and Others *100*

PART FOUR: TRANSFORMATION

  9 Born to Love *119*

  10 Deep Love *133*

  11 Understanding Deep Growth *147*

  12 Cultivating Deep Growth *159*

  13 Suffering Well *171*

  14 Born to Belong *185*

Acknowledgments *199*

Notes *201*

Foreword

Curt Thompson, MD

"THIS NAGGING SENSE OF EMPTINESS." If ever there were five words that distill our current moment's travail, here we have them. If we pull back the curtain to reveal what is behind the burden of our souls, be that the violence on the world stage; the traumas that visit us in our families, schools, and churches; or the unspoken torment swirling in the privacy of our own minds; we will see that the stage on which it all performs is indeed this nagging sense of emptiness—emptiness that itself is rooted in the malignancy of our profound disconnection. Disconnection within and between us has reached its own pandemic proportions, and we are in dire straits, desperately in need of wisdom and guidance to find our way.

Thanks be to God, with *The Connected Life* Todd Hall delivers for us not only a thoughtful, comprehensive understanding of our problem, but also the hope to be found in the biblical narrative as he deftly interweaves it with insights from the fields of neuroscience, psychology, and theology. For indeed, disconnection—as well as its repair and healing—is something that Todd knows about in his bones, and from which he has emerged with good news that we very much need to hear.

When I was first introduced to Dr. Hall and his work, I discovered that here was someone whose giftings were not limited to those of a researcher and teacher of the domains of psychology and Christian spirituality. He is no mere distant observer of these fundamental features of what it means to be human; rather, he is an active and direct participant in the hard work of the life of the soul. Without that, he would be unable to offer you the treasure you hold in your hands. As you will see, there is no stretch of the painful journey of which he speaks—from wounding and isolation to the hope and healing of community—that he has not traveled. Beyond the boundless trove of information about the intersecting fields of neuroscience and spiritual development in which you will soon find yourself immersed, you also will be in conversation with someone who clearly loves those for whom he has written this book. For surely, within the pages you are about to turn, it is as much Todd's kindness as it is his wisdom that will persuade you not only to read these words but to put them into action.

As a psychiatrist working at the intersection of interpersonal neurobiology and Christian spiritual formation, my primary task is to help people tell their stories more truly. This includes walking with them not only as they develop an understanding of what happened to them but also as they imagine a vision for how they will live their lives with confidence and hope in the future. With *The Connected Life*, Todd fluidly and fluently offers us a long-awaited, beautiful rendition for how we can develop that understanding of what has happened to us as well as imagine a vision for transformation in our lives.

From his exploration of our connection crisis, to the neuroscience of relationships and attachment research, and on to his compelling stories of love, deep growth, suffering, and belonging, Todd invites you on a journey that is in no way a simple collection of abstract ideas—no. This is about authentic, embodied change in real time and space. Our time. Our space. Hope and healing for *our* disconnection.

If ever you have questioned if connection were ever again possible, this book answers with a resounding yes! As such, I commend it to you with confidence in Dr. Hall as our guide and in you as his reader. Take your time. You will need it, for the repair of our cultural and personal ruptures of disconnection will take much longer than we would want. But Jesus is not worried. He is too busy being about the hard work of connection—connection that is a hallmark of his kingdom that is here and is surely coming.

Introduction

The Power *of* Loving Connection

As far back as I can remember, my mom suffered from depression and several other psychological disorders. Throughout the course of my mom's life she became relationally disconnected and more physically and emotionally unhealthy—at times even suicidal. This impaired the attachment bond she developed with my sister and me. All this meant that my mom wasn't very emotionally available while I was growing up.

The summer after I finished the fourth grade my mom left our family, and my parents later divorced. I saw her periodically, but she wasn't very involved in my life after that point. This caused a lot of pain and confusion for a nine-year-old boy.

Mirroring a larger US trend, a growing number of families in the 1970s faced a similar situation. I, like most of my friends, grew up in a single-parent family. I didn't know the term back then, but I was a *latchkey kid*. I rode my sky-blue ten speed bike to school and back, and let myself into an empty house after school. Also reflecting a powerful US trend in the 1970s, my family wasn't connected to a church or any community groups, and we didn't live near any extended family. Rather than sharing life with extended family and friends, evenings were filled with an increasing amount of TV-watching. I don't remember the family interacting around the dinner table, but I do remember watching *MASH* with my parents in the fourth grade. For years after my childhood, I felt a sense disconnection from family, friends, and myself.

I realized later that the pain and disconnection I felt in my relationship with God was linked to these formative childhood experiences. Through my college years, in particular, I felt distant from God. I tried to numb the pain by criticizing myself—a subconscious attempt to limit the criticism from important people in my life. In addition, I used my faith as a defense to shield myself from pain. I did this in different ways: trying harder, gaining knowledge about God, and seeking a spiritual high. These approaches, of course, didn't work in the long run. In the end, they simply reinforced my experience of relational disconnection from God and others. This led to a deep sense of emptiness and lack of belonging in my life.

My story reflects our collective story of relational and spiritual disconnection, and the search for meaning in a fragmented, lonely, post-Covid-19 world. Many people feel this uneasy disconnection because the family unit and communities that teach us how to connect to people and to God have steadily weakened over the past fifty years. Sadly, relational and spiritual disconnection are on the rise.

You have likely felt socially and spiritually disconnected, lonely, and empty at times—maybe even a lot of the time. How, then, do you cultivate connection and meaning in the midst of increasing social isolation, loneliness, and fragmentation? Our sense of meaning comes from loving connections with God and others. We are born to connect and we need to belong.

We receive love that ultimately stems from the beautiful love among the Father, Son, and Holy Spirit, which has existed for all eternity. We then give that love out of gratitude for the love we have received; this becomes a virtuous circle. But sometimes we get stuck. There are forces at work in our culture, and in our hearts and habits, that disconnect us from ourselves and others. We may even tell ourselves that we don't need others. It's less painful to strive to make it on our own. But in our most honest moments we know that this is what we want and need: to know and be known, to love and be loved.

I wrote this book for you so that you might overcome this nagging sense of emptiness and cultivate the deep sense of meaning that comes from loving connections with God and the people in your life. Welcome to the journey of the connected life!

PART ONE

The
CONNECTION
CRISIS

1

The Causes *of* Our Connection Crisis

ONE EVENING when I was in the fourth grade, my parents called my sister and me to the living room. This was a rare occurrence, so I knew something important was about to happen. They proceeded to inform us, in a very matter-of-fact manner, that they were separating. My mom would move out and we would stay there with my dad. My parents probably gave some reasons for the separation, but I don't remember what they were. I was struggling to understand what was happening to my world; life would be different from that moment forward.

SIGNS OF A CONNECTION CRISIS

My parents separated in 1979, right at the end of an epidemic period of divorce. My family is a prototypical example from this period. From the outside we were a seemingly normal middle class family living in the suburb of Irvine, California—two parents, two kids, and two cars. On the inside, however, we were a family falling apart and disconnecting from each other, extended family, and community. In Judith Wallerstein's landmark study of the children of divorce, which started in 1971 and spanned twenty-five years, Wallerstein and her colleagues noted: "Since 1970, at least a million children per year have seen their parents divorce—building a generation of Americans that has now come of age."[1] Millions of families were being torn apart—some silently—leaving the children with a legacy of disconnection despite the widespread, misguided belief that children would quickly rebound from divorce and experience no permanent psychological damage. As of the publication of Wallerstein's book in 2000, this group represented one-quarter of the adults in the United States who had reached their forty-fourth birthday.

The rise of divorce is just one indicator of a broader connection crisis in our culture that has emerged over the last fifty years.[2] Over this time period we've also seen a decline in emotional well-being in parallel with decreasing social connection. One trend that illustrates this is the increasing rates of depression in recent decades. Psychologist Martin Seligman stated: "The rate of depression over the last two generations has increased roughly tenfold."[3] Along with depression, we've seen an alarming increase in loneliness in recent decades. In a 2017 article in *Harvard Business Review*, former US surgeon general Vivek Murthy stated, "Loneliness is a growing health epidemic."[4] He goes on to note that, despite being more technologically connected than ever, rates of loneliness have more than doubled since the 1980s. In addition to general social isolation, over half of US adults recently reported feeling like no one knows them well.[5]

There are many interrelated factors that led to our current connection crisis. In some ways they can all be tied back to cultural trends that steadily grew in the last half of the twentieth century—the collective consciousness of the American mind about what constitutes the "good life"—what we might call "the American ideal." This set of ideologies, values, and beliefs that constitute the American ideal include extreme forms of individualism and materialism. This "good life" values independence over friendship, personal comfort over commitment to others, solitary achievements over the common good, and economic success over social and emotional well-being. We can see this set of ideologies in the breakdown of the family and the decline of community—two major trends that have contributed to our connection crisis.

THE FRAGMENTATION OF THE FAMILY STRUCTURE

The family unit, and parent-child relationships in particular, are the most important social context in which children develop attachment bonds. It's in these close relationships that children first learn how to connect to people and God and to develop a sense of morality.

From the mid-1960s through about 1990, the family as a social unit got steadily weaker on numerous counts. The divorce rate more than doubled from 1960 to 1980 (a 136 percent increase). This resulted in large part from dramatic changes in the cultural winds and family law in California in the late 1960s. "A series of statewide task forces," notes Wallerstein, "recommended that men and women seeking divorce should no longer be required to prove that their spouse was unfaithful, unfit, cruel, or incompatible."[6] As a result, in 1969 Governor Ronald Reagan signed the no-fault divorce law into effect, and within a few years no-fault divorce laws spread like a virus throughout all fifty states.

Even before my parents' divorce, their marriage had declined to nothing but a shell of a lifelong partnership. They didn't argue in front of us, but there was a certain emptiness I felt in our family. My parents' relationship wasn't healthy and authentic. I didn't see them express affection toward each other, engage in meaningful dialogue, laugh together, or do things together. This, of course, set the tone for the family; we rarely did things together. As I mentioned, my mom also suffered from emotional and physical illnesses, partly due to the very dysfunctional and fragmented family in which she grew up. The attachment bond developed with my mom was fragile and insecure, and this would come to impact all my significant relationships. The most important social context in which I learned how to connect was unhealthy, which impacted my ability to connect to God and others. Sadly, this is true for millions of Gen Xers and Millennials, and Gen Zers who are now coming of age.

I didn't have to look far to see this same pattern in my friends. In fifth grade, we moved a few houses down from the Peterson family. They had five kids and I became close friends with Johnny and Jeremy. Their family was, in some ways, more dysfunctional than mine. On the surface theirs was also a "normal" middle class family in suburbia, but under the surface was deep fragmentation and chaos. Their mom was an alcoholic, and her alcoholism grew worse as we got older. She was often drunk when I was at the house, and she was verbally and emotionally abusive to her kids. I remember her screaming at the kids and sometimes at me, often for no apparent reason. On a few occasions she threw things at her kids. I remember one afternoon when she threw a frying pan across the room at her son Gary. Thankfully, she missed. The summer after my fifth-grade year, the Petersons divorced. By comparison, I felt my family was calm and "normal." My sister and I lived with my dad who was secure, stable, and calm compared to Mrs. Peterson, but he was still disconnected in some ways. This was the norm I grew up with—divorced, chaotic families filled with all kinds of disconnection.

My experience is a reflection of trends in recent decades related to divorce and family households. The probability of divorce increased steadily from the early 1900s through about 1990 and then plateaued.[7] Even with this plateau, nearly all studies conducted through about 2005 converged in suggesting that the lifetime probability of marital disruption is between 40 percent and 50 percent.[8] In fact, well over half of my childhood friends' parents went through a divorce. Among my inner circle of friends growing up, two-thirds were from divorced families.

A related concerning trend is that two-parent, single-household families declined in the decade of the 2000s.[9] This is due to divorce and increased rates of childbearing in unmarried, cohabiting unions.[10] The level of family dissolution has continued since then due to the fact that informal unions are less stable than marriages.[11]

The breakdown of the family has taken its toll at a societal level. In addition, although the legal act of divorce may be an event, the *effects* of pre-divorce marital conflict and divorce are often long lasting and impact a person's emotional security and sense of connection to God. This was certainly the case for me.

The effects of divorce and family dissolution stem from two sources: changes in family structure (e.g., multiple households, stepparents, lack of contact with non-residential parent), and the relational struggles of parents, which are associated with unhealthy ways of relating to children. I experienced both of these in my own life and have worked with many clients who've experienced these negative effects of divorce. As I mentioned, after my parents' divorce, my sister and I lived with my dad. We would see my mom occasionally on weekends, but we had relatively little contact with her. Life was forever different after the divorce.

The relationship characteristics that predict divorce—domestic violence, frequent conflict, infidelity, weak commitment to marriage, and low levels of love and trust between spouses—all reflect unhealthy relational patterns among parents that presumably get passed down to children in the form of insecure attachment.[12] Attachment relationships (to which we'll return in part three) are relationships in which a child looks to a caregiver to provide physical and emotional comfort in times of distress, and a secure base, or sense of internal security, from which to explore the world. Insecure attachment comes in two basic varieties: (1) *ambivalent*, in which children are highly anxious, and (2) *avoidant*, in which children are emotionally shut down. Both types of insecure attachment are linked to negative developmental and social outcomes later in life, including one's relationship with God.[13] Several fascinating studies have shown that pregnant mothers' attachment tendencies predict their children's attachment tendencies at one year of age, suggesting that attachment is passed down from parent to child through emotional communication and relational interactions.[14]

While there was no violence or infidelity in my parents' case, there was certainly conflict and lack of trust that reflected deeper attachment issues. I know very little of my mom's background because we never visited her extended family, and both her parents died by the time I was two years old. I suspect she experienced a lot of suffering during her childhood. I believe my mom rarely talked about her past with us because it brought up too much unresolved pain. When I tried to have these conversations with her when I was in college and graduate school, she would either fall apart emotionally or get angry. She simply wasn't capable of talking in a coherent and contained way about her past. This incoherence reflects an insecure attachment, which led to significant challenges in our relationship.

Consistent with research on attachment insecurities being passed down, in the past two decades research has generally shown that children with divorced parents, compared with those with continuously married parents, score lower on emotional, behavioral, social, health, and academic outcomes.[15] This corroborates previous findings and indicates that the links between divorce and various aspects of child well-being have remained relatively stable across decades. Young adults with divorced parents also continue to experience negative effects from divorce. While they don't necessarily show higher rates of clinical depression and anxiety, they do continue to experience a significant amount of emotional pain as a result of their parents' divorce.[16]

For example, in one study these young adults reported that they were forced to take on adult responsibilities as a child, felt lonely during childhood, experienced family events and holidays as stressful, felt unsafe at home due to their fathers' absence, missed their fathers, and felt torn between their parents' households.[17] I experienced many of these things as a young adult. I became the peacemaker in my family and took on a parental role with my mom much of the time. Family events and holidays were stressful and brought up a longing for the way things were supposed to be and sadness over the way things were.

The primary functions of the attachment bond—emotional comfort and security—are negatively impacted by the typical experiences of young adults from divorced and dysfunctional homes. This, in turn, has a negative impact on people's experiences of God. If we can't trust our parents, who we can see, to provide emotional support and security, how can we trust God, who we can't see? Patterns of interactions with our attachment figures get stored in our memory as gut-level expectations of how close relationships work. These expectations get placed on our relationship with God, often without realizing it. This doesn't mean that our experiences and expectations of God can't change, but it does mean that the social context in which we are raised profoundly shapes the "God of our gut." And this—not the God of our head—is the God we experience most of the time.

THE DECLINE OF CIVIC AND COMMUNITY GROUPS

Every month my father-in-law, Phil, goes to a local restaurant at o'dark-thirty to meet with a group for breakfast. This group is part of a service club called Lions Clubs International, which was started by a businessman named Melvin Jones. After starting his own insurance agency in 1913, Jones joined a businessmen's luncheon group in Chicago, Business Circle, which was devoted solely to the financial benefit of its members. Jones saw the potential of a group like this and envisioned a broader purpose. He believed that successful business leaders from similar clubs around the country could join forces and put their talents to work to improve their communities. In the summer of 1917, he invited delegates from men's clubs to meet in Chicago and lay the groundwork for a community service organization, and Lions Clubs International was born. One of their main stated purposes is to "take an active interest in the civic, cultural, social, and moral welfare of the community."[18] Today, they run youth and health programs, emphasizing sight (e.g., blindness prevention and vision screenings) and diabetes programs. I admire my father-in-law's involvement in the Lions Club. Every year he helps raise money for sight programs that serve our local community, and I am reminded of the importance of community ties.

Involvement in such service organizations was common among my father-in-law's generation. In contrast, I've never belonged to a service club like this. None of my friends or colleagues in my age group have belonged to one either. Something has shifted in the social fabric of our communities in recent decades.

The family is the most important social group for our emotional, relational, and spiritual development. But we live out family life in a broader social context, which influences our sense of self and emotional and spiritual development directly and indirectly through its influence on family norms. What, then, are the trends with regard to broader social connection in the United States? Sadly, we see a similar weakening of social institutions in the United States over the past fifty years.

Political scientist Robert Putnam's landmark book *Bowling Alone* has documented the eroding effects of declining "social capital" in the United States over the past half-century. Putnam defines social capital as the "connections among individuals—social networks and the norms of reciprocity and trustworthiness that arise from them."[19] He describes the decline in the majority of US social institutions, including political clubs and parties, membership in civic organizations, group recreational activities, religious organizations, unions and workplace associations, philanthropic organizations, and numerous varieties of informal social networks, ranging from card-playing groups to family meals.[20]

This decline cuts across all sectors of American society. For example, we as a nation spent only two-thirds as much time informally socializing at the end of the twentieth century compared to three decades earlier.[21] Likewise, entertaining friends declined by 45 percent over a two-decade period (late 1970s to late 1990s). On one occasion, as I was picking up my son at my in-laws' house, my mother-in-law, Rosa, was canvasing her neighborhood handing out invitations to a coffee get-together at her house. It was noteworthy because hardly anyone does this kind of thing anymore. If this decline in entertaining friends were to continue unabated, Putnam argues, the long-standing social practice of having friends over for dinner would virtually disappear from American life in relatively short order.

Part of this story is also a decline in trust and reciprocity. Beginning in the early 1970s, informal understandings between spouses, business partners, and other parties were no longer trusted. Suddenly, everyone wanted to "get it in writing," giving birth to "preventative lawyering." Trust and connection, it turns out, go hand-in-hand.

Putnam summarized the decline in social connection in this way: "Thin, single-stranded, surf-by interactions are gradually replacing dense, multi-stranded, well-exercised bonds. More of our social connectedness is one shot, special purpose, and self-oriented."[22] Larger groups with long histories, diverse constituents, and multiple objectives (i.e., authoritative communities) are being replaced by smaller groups that "reflect the fluidity of our lives by allowing us to bond easily but to break our attachments with equivalent ease."[23] Place-based social connections are being replaced by function-based social connections; but attachment bonds develop in the context of face-to-face social interactions. The development that occurs in place-based interactions reflects our embodied nature. Our very selves exist in space and time, and the deepest form of relational connection occurs "in person" as it were. Media, through which many function-based social connections now occur, is fundamentally about extending ourselves across space and time. This is reflected in the subtitle of Marshall McLuhan's influential 1964 book, *Understanding Media: The Extensions of Man.*[24] This perspective highlights the notion that we can only extend ourselves so far without a negative impact on deep social connection.

These aspects of decline in social capital are often more pronounced in divorced families, but they have occurred across the board in our society. Many of these trends resonate with my experience and the experiences of my friends growing up. My family wasn't involved in any civic, community, or religious organizations. My dad worked and took care of the household and my sister and me, and that was about it. Divorce typically shatters social relationships maintained by couples. This results in limited contact with would-be friends of the parents and mentors for children. This was the case for my parents—any lasting informal social networks were relatively minimal and thin. It wasn't until I started going to church in the fifth grade with the Peterson family that mentors came into my life. These mentors showed me that God just might be different from my experience of authority figures to that point.

From the late 1990s and into the 2010s, Putnam's thesis was widely debated, leading to some clarifications. On balance, however, there is a general consensus that Putnam was right: social connection significantly declined in the second half of the twentieth century.[25] The causes of this overall trend are complex and difficult to pin down. Putnam, however, suggested four key culprits: (1) time, money, and two-career family pressures; (2) suburbanization, commuting, and sprawl; (3) the rise of electronic entertainment; and most importantly, (4) generational changes.[26]

Putnam's research suggests that, all things considered, the pressures of time, money, and two-career families account for up to 10 percent of the total decline in social connection. Suburbanization, commuting, and sprawl account for an additional 10 percent of the decline. Electronic entertainment—television, and in more recent years the internet—has privatized and individualized our leisure time, accounting for approximately 25 percent. The fourth and most import factor is generational changes: "The slow, steady, and ineluctable replacement of the long civic generation by their less involved children and grandchildren."[27] Although the effects of generational succession vary across different measures of civic engagement, Putnam suggests that this factor may account for up to half of the overall decline in social connection in the United States. This generational change can be explained in part by the national unity and social solidarity brought about by the common cause and adversity of World War II. Generational changes account for such a large portion of the decline because they overlap with shifts in electronic entertainment (or social media) consumption, values, and where and how people experience a sense of community.

The last two factors turn out to be related—in fact, they may be opposite sides of the same coin. The long civic generation was the last cohort of Americans to be raised without television. The more a particular generation was exposed to television during its growing up years, the lower its civic engagement during adulthood. People who grew up in the sixties through the eighties watch television and media more and differently than those raised in the thirties through the fifties. The younger generations watch media more habitually and mindlessly than previous generations, which is linked to lower levels of civic engagement.[28]

These changes reflect a larger societal shift toward individualism and materialism, and away from communal values. This is evident in research on the changing opinions of Americans on what constitutes "the good life."[29] As a generation fades away that is less focused on material goods and more focused on marriage and family, it's being replaced by a cohort that places an increasingly high value on possessions and money (e.g., "a job that pays more than average").

We find further evidence for a shift away from communal values in the networks in which people find a sense of community. People born before 1946 are almost twice as likely as Gen Xers to feel a sense of belonging and connection to their neighborhood, church, local community, and groups and organizations to which they belong.[30] What we see is a narrowing of community connection in the younger generations. Like the long civic generation, Gen Xers still experience a sense of belonging and community with their family, friends, and co-workers. However, they feel less connected to civic communities—neighborhoods, religious organizations, and other organizations.

We're not living our lives in community as much as we used to, and this has contributed to a growing sense of emptiness and lack of meaning in our society and in our lives. Even as the internet makes us more globally minded, our sense of meaning and purpose ultimately comes from living our lives out locally in a community. When I travel, I am reminded of the importance of the community in which I live out my life. I can have all kinds of great ideas about how I want to contribute to society and God's kingdom, but what makes my life meaningful and keeps me spiritually grounded are the people I share life with day in and day out. These are the people that form the community where I feel a sense of belonging, and to whom I am accountable.

My family is the center of this; they know me better than anyone. Walking on this journey with my wife and two sons is a true joy. It's not always easy, but it's deep and life-giving. They also reveal my heart to me in ways that no one else could, because they know me so well and because I am responsible to them in very concrete ways.

My community also extends to my friends, my church and work communities, and my clients. I think of a friend who just went through a difficult career transition and the many hours we spent talking about it. I think of a friend of thirty years and the times we spent together talking about life and encouraging each other. I think about my students, past and present, who have opened their lives to me as they walked through an intense time of training and growth, which is often accompanied by significant emotional pain. I think of various colleagues I work with and the joy of being part of a team focused on the goal of creating real value in the world. I think of my Sunday school class and the way we share life together and support each other during difficult times. I think of my clients who give me the privilege of walking alongside them in their journey, many of them entrusting me with things they've never told anyone in their lives. This is my community; these are the people that give me a sense of belonging and meaning.

Our society is losing the structures that it once had for bringing people together; individuals participate less in long-lasting communities, socialize less, and trust less. A confluence of entangled factors is converging to produce a decline in social connection in the United States over the past fifty years. Boomers, Gen Xers, and Millennials have become more individualistic and materialistic, have less leisure time and more financial pressures, and consume more electronic entertainment in a more mindless way. We are, as a society, more relationally disconnected than we once were. This has negative consequences for our emotional and spiritual well-being.

Numerous indicators of a connection crisis in the West have emerged in the past five decades, including the rise of divorce, the decline of emotional well-being, and the decrease in social connection. Although many factors have contributed to the crisis, an overarching ideology that blends individualism and materialism—what I called the *American ideal*—appears to have paved the way. This ideology manifests itself in two major ways in the social fabric of our lives: the breakdown of the family and the decline of community.

Looking back on my life, it's clear that the social disconnection I experienced growing up contributed to a corresponding spiritual disconnection. There is a close link between the connection crisis in our society and the spiritual disconnection many people experience in their sense of self and relationships with God and others. Unfortunately, there are many effects of this spiritual disconnection, which we turn to in chapter two.

2

The Spiritual Effects *of* Our Connection Crisis

MANY OF MY EARLY RELATIONAL EXPERIENCES left me feeling fundamentally defective in some sense. I wasn't conscious of this feeling a lot of the time, but I developed a set of implicit beliefs about relationships and deep feelings about myself. These included the notion that there was something fundamentally wrong with me, which would always cause others to reject or abandon me in some way. This feeling is what I would now call shame, although I couldn't name it in my early life.

I quickly developed strategies to avoid my emotional pain and secure a kind of pseudo-connection with caregivers and authority figures in my life. The main strategy I landed on was to constantly search for others who might see me for who I truly am in my uniqueness. The subconscious hope was that I would then feel truly known and experience a sense of personal significance.

When I activated this strategy in relationships, however, I often engaged in one of two patterns: (1) I didn't allow others access to my internal world, hoping they would somehow see and validate it without me having to take the risk of revealing it; or (2) I expected too much of others in managing my inner angst. This contributed to people either not perceiving my needs and reaching out or to them withdrawing due to feeling overwhelmed by my emotional turmoil. These strategies might have led to a superficial "pseudo-connection" (meaning, not secure, stable, and healthy) but they sabotaged the goal of a deep, healthy connection characterized by being seen, known, and understood. In striving to manage my pain, I ended up feeling more disconnected.

When we grow up in an environment in which the important relationships in our life are breaking down, how does that affect our relationship with God and our overall spiritual well-being? It would be nice if we could shift into the "spiritual" realm and not deal with patterns of disconnection in our relationship with God. Unfortunately, that's not the way human nature works. It turns out that social disconnection has a profound impact on our experience of God and spiritual community. The connection crisis we're experiencing at a broader societal level reverberates throughout our spiritual lives.

I experienced the link between social disconnection and spiritual disconnection in my own life. Even after I understood intellectually that God had forgiven me, I still felt defective before God. My gut sense was that God simply wouldn't give me the time of day. As in other relationships, I often didn't share my true feelings with God, or I expected God to immediately take my pain away. This led to a painful cycle in which I was left feeling even more distant from God. Those early experiences of social disconnection shaped a strong sense of spiritual disconnection with God and my spiritual communities.

I've observed this link consistently in practicing therapy for twenty-five years. To a person, I've seen my clients' emotional and relational struggles with parents, family members, and communities play out in their relationship with God.

Because we are relational beings, we develop unhealthy relational patterns to protect ourselves from the pain of disconnection and to create a pseudo-connection with the important people in our lives. These patterns may reduce our emotional pain, but they come at great cost. They cut us off from our own emotional truth and create disordered beliefs about how relationships work. These beliefs then drive our relationships and hinder us from being able to connect authentically with others—including God. If we are relational beings, then we would expect the connection crisis in our society to infiltrate into our spirituality because Christian spirituality is all about relationships. Indeed, this is exactly what we see. We see general evidence of spiritual disconnection in research findings on spiritual growth and in research on the spiritual stories of young adults who came of age during increasing societal disconnection.

THE SPIRITUAL DISCONNECTION CRISIS

A recent national study on the current state of discipleship noted that in many churches "there is an assumption that the appropriation of biblical knowledge will by itself lead to spiritual maturity."[1] This assumption, however, appears to be inadequate. Millennials, more so than other generations, desire spiritual growth for the purpose of helping them work through struggles they have experienced.[2] More followers of Christ, especially young adult believers, need emotional healing as an integral part of their spiritual growth process.

The same study also found evidence for an isolationist approach to spiritual growth, at least among those who reported that spiritual growth is important to them, which included most of the Christian adults surveyed (90 percent).[3] Among this group, nearly four out of ten people prefer to pursue spiritual growth on their own (37 percent). In addition, nearly the same percentage (41 percent) believe their spiritual life is "entirely private" and isn't intended to affect one's relatives, friends, communities, or society.

The mindset behind a solitary pursuit of spiritual growth is likely linked to the connection crisis we talked about in chapter one. As the family unit and communities have broken down, the American ideal of individualism has come to permeate the fabric of our spirituality. It has led to many Christians feeling disconnected from God and pursuing life with God on their own.

SPIRITUAL DISCONNECTION AMONG EMERGING ADULTS

One way to examine the association between the connection crisis and spiritual disconnection is to look at the stories of young adults who grew up during a time when social disconnection was already widespread. Two former doctoral students, Kendra Bailey and Brendon Jones, and I conducted a study in which we interviewed emerging adults about their spirituality.[4] We wanted to gain a better understanding of the general themes that characterize the spiritual stories of young Christians. Though we found some positive trends, we also found that many of these young adults were experiencing several forms of spiritual disconnection: guardedness against vulnerability with God, fluctuating connection with God, insecurity with God, disconnection from spiritual community, and difficulty facing spiritual pain. Below I provide a brief window into their stories representing the growing sense of spiritual disconnection.

Guarded against vulnerability with God. Many participants described having difficulty being honest with God. Specifically, they conveyed *feeling guarded against emotional vulnerability with God.* They commonly experienced emotional tension in which they longed to be open and authentic with God, and yet also wanted to protect themselves from expected hurt (e.g., from God's perceived rejection, disappointment, anger, or judgment).

These young adults used or implied a metaphor of building a wall around themselves as protection against feeling unwanted emotions such as shame or sadness. They framed their emotional detachment as a way to defend against the recurrence of painful childhood experiences of disconnection. Even so, participants often discussed their guardedness with God as an unwanted barrier in their intimacy with God.

For example, Allison (all names used for participants from this study are pseudonyms) talked about her defensive style of emotional detachment and how that affected her relationship with God. She described her self-protective wall as unwittingly guarding against authentic emotional experiences with God. Here's how she put it:

I never felt anything spiritual so I was kind of like, *Ok, why am I not feeling anything?* But I think it was kind of, now that I look back, I think it was because I built up that wall. And because I built up that wall, I think God couldn't do anything. I think as the wall is starting to come down, little bit by little bit, I think that he will work in me.

David made an explicit connection between anger experienced regularly with his father and a tentative, cautious relational approach with God:

In high school and before that, my relationship with my dad, . . . he had a temper. We would fight and we were too similar and so we would just not get along ever. With God, I feel like I have to wait and make sure I'm doing everything perfectly right. [I think to myself] *I don't want to pray right now because I'm not really in a place where I can come and be fully there.* I have to tiptoe around. It's really related to how my dad is and like how our relationship is. I've seen that over and over with myself and other people.

Rachel described struggling with experiencing God's love or forgiveness. She identified the roots of her struggle as a self-protective defensiveness against feeling painful emotions that stemmed from childhood hurts. Rachel explained that, in her view, her guardedness against negative emotions unwittingly caused an inability to feel positive emotions in relationship with God:

I mean obviously I'm forgiven and he wants to be forgiving. But I think there are a lot of walls and barriers I have created because of disappointment where I don't think I deserve the forgiveness, and so I'm not willing to receive that from him. Even as I was driving over here today I was thinking, *I know I'm forgiven. He wants me to feel that, but I'm not allowing myself to feel that yet because I'm so disappointed with certain things that happened.* Because of my experiences, a lot of the ways I learned to cope . . . was by turning off my emotional capacity. Sometimes it was so painful to feel that it was easier not to feel at all. So something God is trying to heal in me is teaching me how to feel again. Something I think I will probably always struggle with is feeling truly loved or feeling forgiven or feeling those things between us.

Fluctuating connection with God. Most of the young adults described a fluctuating sense of connection in their relationship to God. Sometimes they experienced God as close, but other times they experienced God as distant; sometimes they felt loved by God, while at other times they felt nothing from God. These fluctuations occurred with regular frequency, on a weekly or even daily basis. Participants had different interpretations of what caused these fluctuations, including God's actions, their own actions, or simply the normal rhythms of spiritual life. They also had various strategies for responding during times of perceived disconnection from God.

For example, some participants engaged in more spiritual activities and tried vigorously to restore a sense of felt connection to God, whereas others engaged in fewer spiritual practices and adopted a more passive, resigned stance. Regardless, they commonly reported experiencing negative emotions in response to feeling disconnected from God (e.g., discouragement, disappointment, sadness, anger, and doubt).

Beth, for example, described her experience of God's presence as alternating between closeness and distance. Her metaphor of a Slinky is perhaps the most apt description for this theme:

> I feel like [experiencing God's presence] is like a Slinky. It goes back and forth and back and forth. I feel like that's on me.

Mary talked about spiritual emotions as sometimes present in her experience, while at other times absent. This was particularly true in regard to the emotion of love:

> There will be times when [I think], *I know God loves me.* I just don't question it. And then there are times where I'm like, *I wish I could feel your love, why can't I feel your love?*

Insecurity with God. Given the fluctuations in felt connection to God, it's not surprising that most of these young adults experienced emotional insecurity in their perceived relationship to God. Such experiences of insecurity were typically accompanied by negative emotions such as anxiety, worry, fear, inadequacy, guilt, shame, confusion, or feeling unloved. For example, Sarah's discussion of her spiritual life was filled with descriptions of questioning her own adequacy. Here is how she described it in her own words:

> I often have that feeling I'm not doing enough. "What more do I need to do?" And I was kind of basing that off of not feeling a change in my life based on the things I was doing. So I was definitely like, "Am I growing enough? Am I doing the right thing? What more do I need to do?" More, more, more. And then coming to the realization that that's not a good view to take.

Sarah appears to have chronically questioned her self-adequacy in her relationship with God. In fact, when we asked her how often she has these feelings, she stated:

> I would say the majority of the time, at least in the past. And I don't know what is to come [in the future] but probably most of my life I've felt like that.

Like many emerging adults we interviewed, Sarah spoke of her feelings of anxious inadequacy as a core experience in her relationship with God.

For a number of emerging adults, insecurity took the form of not feeling loved by God. They articulated how failures in their past relationships with family and friends negatively impacted their ability to experience God's love, which in turn made it difficult to take ownership over their faith. For example, Allison stated:

> Yeah, I'm starting to own my faith. Obviously God has blessed me. I'm grateful and thankful to him for that. He's a great God. I have, because of my issues with friends and family and stuff, felt

not loved. Just this last year, I didn't really realize it would kind of be like, "Oh yeah, God still loves the world." You know the verse, John 3:16, but I never really personally felt like God loved me as an individual, and just through this last year, and through the church I've been attending down here, I've kind of been waking up to that fact and how I've kind of built a wall and how I'm blocking God out because of how I've been hurt as a kid.

Feeling disconnected from spiritual community. Some of the young adults we interviewed described feeling generally disconnected from spiritual community. Debbie put it this way:

> I never had a level of accountability in my walk, and . . . felt like I didn't have real fellowship or anyone coming alongside me. We had a church family, but it was just people we ate together with or did stuff together with . . . There was nothing deeper I guess.

Another participant, Lizzie, described it this way:

> We looked around for other churches, and so there would be weeks where we wouldn't go to church and other times we would go to church, but it would be in these foreign places where I didn't know anybody and felt like a total outsider. . . . And so I think eventually sometime during high school we just stopped going. . . . And that totally, I think probably in a lot of ways, stagnated my growth spiritually, [that] removal from the church because it had been so much a foundational influence in my life growing up. And I think that probably had the effect of just feeling deprived of relationship and community in my church.

Difficulty facing spiritual pain. Finally, another prominent theme that emerged from our participants was the presence of pain, hardship, and suffering, particularly in their relationship to God. The participants' stance toward pain distinguished a less spiritually mature group from a more spiritually mature group, but everyone we interviewed discussed facing difficulties both spiritually and in other areas of life.

One participant clearly summarized this theme when asked if there was anything related to the spiritual lives of young adults that the interview hadn't covered:

> I've just been noticing that people are suffering. College-aged students are suffering. And I think I've noticed that in my friends, and hearing friends talk about friends, and experiencing that myself. . . . We just don't know how to deal with [pain] because our culture is such a "get it right now, don't feel pain, mask the pain" [culture]. We don't know how to sit with pain and work through that well, and I know there are people that have done that well.

The less mature young adults tended to minimize, avoid, or mask their pain, though not everyone exhibited this pattern. As noted, we found a more mature group of young adults who seemed to accept, embrace, and acknowledge their pain. However, this pattern of minimizing spiritual pain did stand out as a common theme.

All of the participants were coping with pain in various ways, but differences emerged in their level of defensiveness. The more immature participants showed defenses that disavowed, distorted, or inhibited their experiences of spiritual pain. For these emerging adults, it was almost as if pain were incompatible with their faith. These participants chose adjectives to describe their relationship with God that were inconsistent with their actual narratives, probably to compensate for rejection, disappointment, and struggle they had faced in their human relationships and in their relationship with God.[5] For example, Allison chose the word *omniscient* as an adjective to describe her relationship with God. When asked why she chose this word, she stated that she couldn't understand why her family wasn't able to find a church. She seemed to be using the omniscience of God as a way to avoid a sense of disappointment from not being able to find a church.

Others in the less mature group also chose adjectives that seemed to compensate for their spiritual pain. Some participants didn't seem to be aware of the ways they minimized their pain. Their positive adjectives weren't congruent with the more negative emotional tone of their memories. Others were more consistent in their descriptions, yet they described their relationship with God in an overly idealistic way. While this group of less mature young adults exhibited a range of defenses to mask their pain, there was still a theme of difficulty directly facing and working through spiritual pain.[6] A deep and authentic connection with God is hindered by hiding pain, even if unconsciously.

Christians throughout history have experienced times of disconnection and fluctuation in their relationship with God. However, the common occurrence of these themes among our young adult interviewees illustrates an emerging trend of spiritual disconnection and the impact of growing up with increasing rates of social disconnection. Throughout these themes and interviews we see a strong link between disconnection with God and painful experiences of disconnection in childhood. Often these young adults told us they believed that their current experiences of disconnection with God were rooted in emotional pain, isolation, conflict, and ultimately disconnection with their caregivers.

This corroborates the link between the broader connection crisis and a growing sense of spiritual disconnection among many Christians. Our earliest relational experiences with caregivers form implicit templates in our mind for how important relationships work. It makes sense, then, that increasing rates of disconnection in our families and communities are translating into higher rates of spiritual struggle and disconnection from God and spiritual communities.

Social disconnection has a profound impact on our experience of God and spiritual community. The connection crisis in our society has led to a spiritual connection crisis. We all develop strategies (albeit mostly unconscious) to cope with the emotional pain of disconnection and to maintain pseudo-connections to the important people in our lives.

These strategies, or defense mechanisms, inevitably backfire and hinder the very connection we most want and need. This happens because the strategies require us to sacrifice something necessary for healthy relationships: connection to ourselves. We do this in all kinds of ways, although there are broad patterns in terms of how we cope with pain (discussed further in part three). When we are unaware of these patterns, allowing them to operate on autopilot, they hinder our spiritual growth. To further complicate matters, as believers these strategies often play out in the context of our spiritual life. They have the same defensive function and the same negative effects, but they can be more difficult to see, shrouded in spiritual accomplishments and experiences that look very positive on the surface. In chapter three we'll take a look at three ways we inhabit our spirituality that can actually lead us astray and cause disconnection from God and others.

3

Misguided Spirituality

I BECAME A CHRISTIAN the same summer my mom left the family. There were several ways I tried to use spirituality to find meaning in my fragmented family life. Of course our life with God should be the primary place we find meaning, but I searched for it in misguided ways. Although these approaches are different on the surface, they're based on the motivation to control rather than connect. I wasn't aware of it at the time, but I was trying to control things to produce a sense of meaning and prevent emotional pain.

There are three misguided approaches I used at different times in my early Christian life, and still default to at times. I think we all use variations of these approaches. Although they may work superficially in the short term, they don't actually increase our connection, love, or sense of meaning. Instead, they leave us feeling more isolated and alone. This is not a comprehensive framework, but these approaches are meant to illustrate how we use our spirituality in misguided ways. The three approaches I highlight here focus on trying harder (the willpower approach), knowing more (the intellectual approach), and feeling better (the spiritual-emotional high approach).[1]

THE WILLPOWER APPROACH

One of the ways I tried to find meaning in the midst of my fragmented family life was to work really hard in my spiritual life. I call this the *willpower approach*. I thought if I just tried hard enough, gave God everything I had, and "performed" well spiritually, I would find a sense of meaning and all the pain would go away. For years my spirituality was fueled by my own willpower and focused on performance. I read the Bible and prayed every day, attended every church event possible, took a leadership role in our youth group, went on short-term missions trips, and even directed the youth group the summer after my freshman year of college. As a high school student, I became the right-hand person for the youth pastors who worked there during that time. I was the recognized youth leader, and this was my "reward in full."

But when I got to college it all started to fall apart, because God gave me a roommate who worked even harder. This really irritated me. Joe was a paragon of virtue and discipline. He told me that when he started high school he decided he was going to do two things: get a perfect GPA and lead his basketball team to win the state championship. And, of course, he accomplished both of these goals. He made it sound easy—you just decide to do it, and then do it. It was as simple as that—for him.

Joe approached his spirituality the same way. He was passionate and disciplined about his spirituality. He spent long hours studying the Bible. What irritated me the most was that he would often spend all night praying instead of sleeping, as lower spiritual life forms, like me, had the bad habit of doing. I would occasionally wake up in the middle of the night, and there would be Joe, on his knees hunched over his bed in our dorm room, praying. *The nerve of that guy*, I would think to myself. *How dare he pray all night and make me feel guilty for sleeping!* I wasn't about to give up my sleep for God.

As much as I wanted to blame Joe for my guilt and irritation, it really wasn't his fault. I was to blame for my irritation—and it gradually revealed my heart. Someone who seemed ahead of me on the spiritual journey (as if it were a contest) forced me to realize that I was really seeking praise and recognition. I sought these things to keep my pain below the surface. This meant I was somewhat cut off from my emotions and, because of this, detached from God. The unintentional net result of my pursuit of meaning kept God at a distance and continued to leave me feeling empty inside.

If you're a follower of Christ, it's natural and good to turn to God to find a sense of meaning. Putting effort into our relationship with God is certainly a good thing. But sometimes the *way* we approach our spirituality backfires and ends up leading to more disconnection and emptiness.

In addition to experiencing this myself, I've worked with many clients who engage in this misguided approach. It leaves them frustrated and empty, because there is something deeper going on in their heart that is hindering their connection with God and others.

THE INTELLECTUAL APPROACH

Trying harder isn't the only approach to meaning I've taken or seen among my clients. I also focused a lot of energy on gaining knowledge *about* God and the Bible—the *intellectual approach*. I believed, deep in my heart, that if I knew enough about God and Scripture in my head, I would find meaning and the pain from my family would go away. Somewhere along the way I developed this implicit belief. I read and studied Scripture, read theological works and commentaries, and attended a Christian college where I completed a minor in biblical and theological studies.

At first I was excited about what I was learning about God, even with my anxious striving under the surface. But over time things changed, and by the middle of college the excitement had worn off. I gradually entered into a dry season in my spiritual life. The knowledge about God felt empty because I didn't feel God's presence. Focusing on concepts about God kept my pain away in the short run, but at the cost of connection with God.

I've seen clients and students over the years use this approach—often without being aware of it. Connor, an undergraduate student, came to see me for therapy when he had a crisis of faith. He was a bright philosophy major and had gained a lot of knowledge about God and theology. Connor had some of the same struggles I experienced years before. His main reason for coming to therapy was that he didn't feel God's presence. He became so frustrated and desperate that at one point he gave God an ultimatum: "God, you have one week to show up in a way that I can feel your presence." That week came and went and Connor felt nothing—no trace of God to be found. So, Connor informed me, he had given up on God and he wasn't sure if he was a Christian any longer.

As I tried to help Connor unpack his internal conflict, it was difficult to access any feelings he was having. He even reported his struggle over not feeling God's presence in a fairly matter-of-fact way. He brought up theological doctrines to engage me in intellectual conversations and debate; when I tried to shift conversation to his experience, he would quickly return to the intellectual level. It was difficult to feel a sense of connection with Connor, because he was protecting himself from a painful vulnerability around his relationship with his distant, angry father. Even though Connor wanted to experience God's presence, he continued to focus on ideas about God to keep his pain away.

Learning about God is a necessary and important part of finding meaning in our spiritual journey, but it's not enough by itself. If we make the pursuit of information about God our ultimate goal, it creates a negative cycle of disconnection and emptiness.

THE SPIRITUAL-EMOTIONAL HIGH APPROACH

In addition to trying harder and focusing on knowledge about God, there were times I pursued the *spiritual-emotional high approach*. Every summer in high school I went to a camp in the mountains with my youth group. As with most camps, we had competitions, played games, worshiped together, and heard compelling talks from great speakers. Every summer

I would experience a spiritual high, which helped to numb my emotional pain. I sought these spiritual highs again and again to stay one step ahead of my pain. I pursued a spiritual high through camps, mission trips, worship experiences, and sometimes through helping and serving others.

I'm not sure if I loved God and others more, but I felt good—at least on the surface. In my heart I thought, *If I can just hang on to this spiritual high, then I'll find meaning and all this pain will go away*. But it didn't work; the high would wear off and the pain and emptiness would return, leaving me feeling like a spiritual failure.

I have worked with many people operating from this approach. For some, it takes the form of pursuing an intense experience of God in order to feel a spiritual high that numbs their pain. For others, it takes a subtler form of losing one's self (and the pain) through recognition gained from incessantly helping others. This was the case with Rebecca. She came to see me due to a low-grade depression, or malaise. She couldn't pin down exactly why she was feeling this way, but it was starting to affect her functioning. Rebecca was involved in numerous ministries at her church and was constantly helping others.

She was known as someone with a servant's heart who would always step in to help. This is true, and it's one of Rebecca's strengths; but our strengths are often a mirror image of our weaknesses. Rebecca sought a kind of spiritual high—whether it was stepping in to teach, mentoring younger women, spearheading an event, or supporting someone during a crisis, she got a spiritual buzz from the praise she received from helping others. Buried beneath all of this was a deep fear of not being worthy of love. This was the main cause of her low-grade depression, but she couldn't gain access to these feelings because her compulsive caregiving kept them below the surface of her awareness. When the buzz wore off and people returned to their lives, she was left feeling unsure of who she was and felt very alone. Others didn't know Rebecca at a deeper level because she didn't really know herself. In addition, people in her life often didn't reach out to meet her needs partly because she projected an image of self-sufficiency. In the end, seeking a spiritual high from serving others left Rebecca feeling more disconnected from God and others in her life.

As with Rebecca, for people operating in this mode, the high usually wears off and the emptiness and deeper relational issues resurface. It doesn't lead to deep change. In fact, none of these approaches lead to a deeper sense of meaning in our spiritual journey. We're prone to use our spirituality to disconnect from emotional pain, which then disconnects us from ourselves, others, and God, leading to a feeling of inner fragmentation. If we're supposed to turn to God to find meaning but these approaches don't work, then how *do* we find meaning in this socially fragmented world?

THE RELATIONAL APPROACH

During my junior year in college, something strange happened. A lifetime of pain was crashing in on all my relationships, and I just couldn't make them work. Also, no matter how hard I tried, I felt empty and distant from God. It was probably the first time, but certainly not the last, that I came to the end of myself. I realized I was trying to take this spiritual journey alone and that I needed God and the people in my life to help me.

Inside my soul, I turned to God; it was the last move I had. And God showed up. One day after some relationships had fallen apart, I was wandering around my college campus, confused and sad, and I wandered into our campus chapel for no apparent reason. Someone was speaking and I sat down in the back for a few minutes. To this day, I have no idea who was speaking or what the topic was. But the speaker said something, and through it, I heard God speaking to me. What I heard was something like this: *There are some things inside of you that you need to face, and you need me and others to help you. I will be with you and I will guide you.*

That experience put me on a path toward a fourth approach to finding meaning. That day, I began a process of opening myself up to God in new ways and reaching out to others in my life. It was scary.

But God was present and he used some wonderful friends, mentors, and therapists to help me heal and grow.

The fourth approach to finding meaning is the *relational approach* that involves living a connected life—a life in which our spirituality empowers us to face our pain with the help of loving relationships, and to develop more authentic relationships with God and others.

The other three approaches are good, insofar as they go: being intentional and putting effort into our spiritual life is critical. Likewise, it's crucial to understand who God is, how he created us, and how we are designed to live and flourish. And experiencing the high of true spiritual growth and caring for others is essential. But if we pursue these things apart from relationship—apart from loving God and our neighbor—they will fall short. Paul reminds us in 1 Corinthians 13 that without love, we gain nothing.

The relational view flows from our understanding of the radical relationality of our triune God, and it's being confirmed and elaborated in amazing ways by scientific research. When we consider *how* we become more loving, theology and scientific disciplines ranging from neuroscience to attachment theory are converging in suggesting that it occurs in and through relationships with God and others.

We are loved into loving. To find meaning and grow spiritually, we must open ourselves to be loved into loving. There is no other way. Being loved into loving is the only antidote to the disconnection we're now experiencing at a societal level and in our individual lives. We must understand how relationships work and fully engage in them if we are going to experience deep meaning and transformation, and ultimately grow into the image of Christ.

Our relationships cause us the most joy and the most pain in our lives, and that is not accidental. It's precisely because God made us for relationships. Relationships are outside of our direct control, and so they can cause a lot of confusion, frustration, and emptiness. At the same time, relationships are what give our lives meaning, purpose, and vitality. They are what make us human because God designed us for connection.

Fast forward to today—I'm blessed with good friendships, a healthy marriage of twenty-nine years, good relationships with my two sons and other family members, and a supportive spiritual community. My relationship with God, like all relationships, has its ups and downs, but I have a deepening trust in God and gratitude for his amazing sacrifice for me. I still experience struggles, to be sure, but there is no doubt that I am a changed person compared to my earlier years. I grew from an inner emptiness to a growing sense of connection and meaning in my life. And I've been privileged to guide many others on this journey through the process of psychotherapy.

How does this happen? It happens through loving connection. I was, and continue to be, loved into loving by God and by many wonderful people in my life. Through experience, I've learned that being connected to others in a meaningful way is essential to human well-being, and in our fragmented, distanced world it only happens with intentionality. Loving connection fosters a deep sense of meaning and helps us become more loving and Christlike.

John tells us that we love others because God first loved us (1 John 4:19). Paul also reminds the Corinthian believers that God "comforts us in all our troubles so that we can comfort others" (2 Corinthians 1:4). This is the positive spiral of love. We see evidence for this same positive spiral in the social sciences. As we'll see, we take in others' emotions and love through emotional communication. Secure, or healthy attachment is passed down in this way from parent (or any attachment figure) to child. We are indeed loved into loving.

There are three misguided approaches to our spirituality that don't work in the long run: the willpower approach, the intellectual approach, and the spiritual-emotional high approach. Although these approaches are entirely understandable, they will leave you empty as they short-circuit relational connection with God and others. There is, however, a fourth approach that will help you find meaning in a fragmented world—the relational approach that involves living a connected life. My hope is that this book will help you become better equipped to live a connected life and find a deep sense of meaning in this disconnected and fragmented world. We begin in part two with relational knowledge.

PART TWO

RELATIONAL
KNOWLEDGE

4

We Know More Than We Can Say

IN THE MOVIE *Good Will Hunting*, Will Hunting (played by Matt Damon) is a math genius who suffers from the effects of being abused as a foster child. We see these effects play out with Will's love interest, Skylar. He is afraid of intimacy because emotional closeness might reveal the pain he's been carrying his entire life, so he keeps Skylar at arm's length. He is reluctant to allow her into his world, and he lies about his past. When it comes to relationships, Will is anything but a genius.

A professor at MIT discovers his intellectual genius and wants to take Will under his wing. When Will gets in trouble with the law, Professor Lambeau appeals to the judge to release Will into his custody, provided that Will go to therapy. After Will sabotages the first few therapies, Lambeau begs an estranged former classmate, Sean Maguire (played by Robin Williams), to see Will. As a psychology professor and therapist, Sean agrees.

In one scene, Will speculates about Sean's inner demons trying to break him down in another attempt to sabotage a therapy relationship.

Being intellectually gifted and observant, his deductions hit on a nerve when he tells Sean, "You married the wrong woman." Sean grabs Will by the throat and pushes him up against a bookshelf. This statement got under his skin because Sean's wife had died of cancer.[1] Ironically, Will doesn't use his intellectual knowledge to navigate life with wisdom. Instead, he uses it to defend himself against emotional pain, damaging relationships with people who care about him.

Like Will, we mess up relationships despite our intellectual knowledge about how relationships work and how we should live. There's often a split between our intellectual knowledge and our relational knowledge. Even worse, we sometimes use our intellectual knowledge in ways that hurt our relationships. As I did in my early Christian life—and still do sometimes—we use head knowledge to push away pain and the people who love us most. The question of course is, *why?* Why does Will do this? Why do we do this, even when it hurts our own well-being? And what can we do to prevent misusing our intellectual knowledge?

GOD, MAYBE YOU GAVE UP ON ME?

Julia, a student I interviewed for a research project, described her family life growing up as "crazy." Her family was poor, and she experienced a lot of neglect and trauma. Beginning in junior high, she attended youth group regularly and several spiritual mentors invested in her life. Despite this foundation, she hit an "empty and dark" period during high school. She became increasingly aware of a disconnect between her explicit knowledge of God and her experience of God. She began to feel distant from God. At first, she coped with it by pushing it down and acting as if she felt close to God. She gradually began putting on a persona of the spiritual leader everyone thought she was. But it started to wear on her because, deep down, she knew everything was not okay between her and God.

This turned out to not just be a bad week, month, or year. For five years she felt like she was wandering in the darkness, with no sense of

connection to God. In the interview, she conveyed how she cried out
to God at camp when this all came to a head:

> God, I can't do this anymore. It's been five years. You know that's
> a long time. Maybe this isn't really real anymore. Maybe I did
> something wrong and you've left me. Maybe you gave up on me.

Some spiritual leaders would tell you that Julia had this experience
because she lacked knowledge about God or was spiritually disengaged
—if she didn't feel close to God, she must not understand God and his
grace. But this wasn't the case. This conventional explanation, while
certainly a factor at times, doesn't fit Julia's situation. She was very
involved in her church and spiritual community. She regularly engaged in spiritual practices, and she had a solid understanding of the
Bible. Julia knew a lot about God for someone her age.

This explanation rests on the assumption that our relationship with
God is fundamentally different from our relationship with other
humans because God is perfect. In my early years as a Christian, I believed this. Perhaps, says this line of thought, our relationship with God
operates in a different matrix. Of course our relationship with God is
different in certain respects, because we are relating to an all-knowing,
all-powerful, all-loving God; in human relationships, both parties are
fallen, finite, and culpable for ongoing difficulties. But this isn't the case
in our relationship with God. So it's not too hard to get from there to
the idea that we should always feel close to God, that we should always
trust God, that we should never doubt His love, that we should never
feel abandoned by God. But Julia did; and sometimes we do too. How
can we know so much about God, yet feel so far away?

RELATIONAL KNOWLEDGE

Relational knowledge is about a very simple and powerful idea. The best
way to understand why we struggle with emotional intimacy—keeping
God and others at arm's length—is to think of these patterns as beliefs
we carry in our emotions and relationships. Knowing how to relate to

God and others—how to love—is a distinct kind of knowledge that is very different from intellectual, or explicit, knowledge. Our society doesn't put a high value on relational knowledge, but it may be the deepest reality of our human experience and the clearest path toward meaning.

Will Hunting's troubled relationships, despite his genius, and Julia's "empty and dark" period with God are textbook examples of relational knowledge in action. Although they are very different stories they share a basic underlying pattern—disordered relational knowledge existing despite strong, even genius level, explicit knowledge.

Will sabotages his relationship with Sean; his disordered relational knowledge tells him that authority figures don't really care and eventually will hurt him, so it's better to hurt them first even if he has to use his intellectual knowledge for that purpose. This is what Will's mind and soul know about how relationships work based on his past experience, and this is very real in a certain sense. He doesn't know that anything different is possible.

In the next therapy session, Sean takes Will to a park, attempting to break through to Will one last time by highlighting the stark contrast between his extraordinary intellectual knowledge and his impoverished relational knowledge. He is inviting Will into a relationship that will bring healing and growth in his relational knowledge. As they sit at a park in front of a scenic pond, Sean looks at Will and says:

> I ask you about love . . . you'll probably quote me a sonnet. But you've never looked at a woman and been totally vulnerable. Knowing someone that could level you with their eyes. Feeling like God put an angel on earth just for you; who could rescue you from the depths of hell. And you wouldn't know what it's like to be her angel; to have that love for her be there forever . . . through anything . . . through cancer. And you wouldn't know about sleeping sittin' up in a hospital room for two months holding her hand because the doctors could see in your eyes that the terms "visiting hours" don't apply to you.

You don't know about real loss, because that only occurs when you love something more than you love yourself. I doubt you've ever dared to love anybody that much. . . . But you're a genius, Will. No one denies that.

You're an orphan, right? Do you think I'd know the first thing about how hard your life has been; how you feel; who you are, because I read *Oliver Twist?* Does that encapsulate you?

Personally, I don't care about all that. Because you know what? I can't learn anything from you I can't read in some . . . book.[2]

Regardless of how much Will knows *explicitly* about love, relationships, or the human condition, it won't change his relational competence until that knowledge becomes personal and he learns how to love and relate in a healthy way. Relational knowledge can be disordered, and even extraordinary explicit knowledge by itself won't transform it. In fact, it can be used to damage it.

At the end of their conversation in the park, Sean tells Will that if he's willing to talk about himself, then Sean's in—he's fascinated, engaged, and wants to help.

"But you don't want to do that, do ya' sport?" Sean continues. "Because you're afraid of what you might say."

Will knows there is pain in his soul, but he cannot yet speak of it. He knows he needs to protect himself from emotional closeness, but he doesn't know why. And even if he did, it's not the kind of knowledge that can be fully captured in a concept. This is what psychoanalyst Christopher Bollas calls "unthought knowns."[3] We truly know more than we can say.

Julia's relational struggles with God happened for the same reason as Will's: disordered relational knowledge based on painful experiences from her past. Julia had trouble trusting God due to the neglect and turmoil she experienced in her closest attachment relationships. She knew the Bible and essential Christian doctrine, and she was very involved in church. But she carried inside her a deep feeling of abandonment. Julia told me that she experienced poverty, trauma, neglect, and "deep hurt" growing up. She felt that her parents were not there for her. Julia developed an insecure attachment to her parents. This was the basis for her relational knowledge of how to relate to others. This relational knowledge heavily filtered her experience of God. Julia felt God had left her.

Julia's relational knowledge told her that the people she was supposed to rely on (e.g., parents and God) didn't really care about her. They would hurt her and eventually leave her, at least emotionally if not physically as well. This is what Julia expected of important relationships at a deep gut level. Because of this, she had an emotional block to experiencing God's love. It was like there was no hook in her heart on which to hang God's love. To protect herself against imminent abandonment, Julia developed ways of pushing people away, including God. All of this caused deep struggles in loving God and loving her neighbor. Julia knew a lot about God in her head, but she didn't know God on a relational level. This is the knowledge split we all experience in some way.

What can we do to heal and grow our relational knowledge of loving God and neighbor, and in this find meaning in the connections for which we were created? We need to understand two distinct ways of knowing and how they become split apart, even in our relationship with God.

Two Ways of Knowing

The Getty Villa in Malibu, California, houses J. Paul Getty's stunning antiquities collection. Greek statues dating back to the BC era line many of the rooms. In September 1983, an art dealer showed up at the Getty wanting to sell them a statue for $10 million. A group of scientists from the Getty studied the statue for fourteen months and concluded that it was the real deal. But a number of experts in Greek sculpture looked at the statue and in one glance concluded that it didn't look quite right—that there was something wrong with this statue.

Well, who was right? It turned out that the experts in Greek sculpture were right.[4] Within seconds of looking at the statue, the experts gained a better understanding of the statue than the Getty scientists had with fourteen months of high-tech investigations. It was because these experts had spent thousands of hours in direct contact with Greek statues. They didn't just know *about* these statues; they knew them in a more intimate way. This is what Malcolm Gladwell refers to as *thin slicing*—the ability of our gut-level senses to find patterns in situations and behavior based on very narrow slices of experience.[5]

This story illustrates how our brains process information in two very different ways: a conscious, slow, deliberate way, and a rapid, automated way outside our conscious awareness. In other words, there are two qualitatively different ways of knowing, and understanding how they each work, both independently and in tandem, is crucial for finding meaning and growing spiritually.

We know some things through ideas—the conscious deliberate strategy that the Getty scientists used. They looked at precise data about the statue and deduced logical conclusions from the data. This was the way Julia knew God loved her when she hit the empty and dark period in her life. It was something she knew about God in her head rather than something she experienced with God.

We often refer to this as *head knowledge*, but scholars also refer to it as rational, propositional, conceptual, analytical, verbal, or explicit knowledge. *Explicit knowledge* is linear, logical, and language based. In this type of knowledge, you know something based on logic or concepts, and you can put it into words easily. Scientists also refer to this kind of knowledge as "knowing that." Julia, for example, "knew that" God loved her. This way of knowing is processed in particular systems in the brain, primarily in the top (cortex) left regions of the brain. Although there is overlap, these are somewhat distinct systems from those that process *implicit knowledge*, suggesting that they are qualitatively different ways of knowing. These two types of knowledge are processed differently in the brain, consistent with the fact that we experience these ways of knowing differently.

While we know some things through ideas and logic, we know other things through our experiences, physiological responses, feelings, and intuition—sometimes without knowing *how* we know these things. This kind of knowledge goes by various names, such as personal knowledge, tacit knowledge,[6] experiential knowledge, gut-level knowledge, and the term I'll use, *implicit knowledge*. All of our experience is filtered through the lens of our gut-level or "implicit" processing. This kind of knowing is nonlinear, holistic, doesn't exist in words, and is based on emotion. We get a feeling in our gut that provides evaluative information about a situation, much like the feeling the experts had when they looked at the statue.

Implicit knowledge includes bodily or "procedural" knowledge, such as knowing how to shoot a basketball. Someone may know the principles of how to shoot a basketball really well—for example, you're supposed to lock your elbow and snap your wrist as you shoot the ball. But that same person may not be able to actually shoot a basketball well at all. This is because their body may not know how to shoot a basketball. They may not have the right kind of implicit or procedural knowledge to actually make the ball go in the hoop. This is why athletes spend more time practicing than discussing theories about their sport (although explicit understanding shapes training). In addition to knowing *how* to do things in our body, implicit knowledge includes reading others' feelings through micro expressions, which is illustrated when we sense someone is lying to us.

LIE TO ME: IMPLICIT KNOWLEDGE AND MICRO EXPRESSIONS

The show *Lie to Me* illustrates the contrast between explicit knowledge and implicit knowledge or *thin slicing*.[7] The show's main character, Dr. Cal Lightman, is an expert in detecting deception. He analyzes facial expressions, body language, and tone of voice to determine when people are lying and why. He uses these skills to help law enforcement and government agencies uncover the truth.

Lightman's character is loosely based on a real psychologist named Paul Ekman.[8] Dr. Ekman is a pioneer in identifying distinct emotions from facial expressions that are found in most cultures. He became so good at identifying facial expressions that he began consulting with law enforcement agencies to help them detect lies.

Lightman demonstrated both kinds of knowledge in the show. He had extensive explicit knowledge of micro expressions and the Facial Action Coding System that Ekman developed. He often explained to his clients how he knew someone was lying. For example, when accusing someone of a crime, the person would respond seemingly calmly but would exhibit a micro expression of anger. This is a facial expression displayed too rapidly to clearly see, but your emotions detect it. Lightman would often show his clients the facial expression in slow motion and explain why people respond this way when they feel caught or trapped in a lie. The explanation is explicit knowledge— conceptual understanding of how to detect lies and how people tend to behave when they lie.

In a real-life example of this, Ekman shows a slow-motion replay of Kato Kaelin responding to a question by District Attorney Marcia Clark in the infamous O. J. Simpson case. At one point in the interrogation, Clark asks Kaelin: "Mr. Kaelin, you got a lot of money for your appearance on *Current Affair*, didn't you?" Kaelin calmly answers, "Yes," as he leans forward, and you don't see any clear facial expression. However, when you slow the tape down you see Kaelin make a facial expression that Ekman calls *scorn*—a combination of anger and disgust—in which Kaelin wrinkles his nose and tightens his upper lip. (You can find this video by searching online.) He looks like an animal growling.

While Lightman can explain the micro expressions associated with lying (explicit knowledge), he can also masterfully read people's emotions in real time, without the benefit of slow-motion replay. He can go out in the field and interrogate someone and discern whether that person is lying by his gut-level senses—by thin slicing. This more direct form of knowledge about lying is implicit knowledge. Lightman—and Ekman—have trained their emotions to be a finely tuned instrument that reflects the feelings of others. When an alleged criminal exhibits micro expressions, Lightman senses this in his own emotional responses. This, first and foremost, is how he "knows" someone is lying. A narrow view of knowledge that equates science—which is code for quantification and logic—with knowledge would have us believe that Lightman's gut-level emotional responses don't count as knowledge. This, however, is an incomplete view of knowledge.

We may not be experts at detecting lies, but we instinctually sense people's emotions every day. We often talk about having a gut feeling about something. What we mean is that we think we know something, but either we have no idea how we know it, or we can't easily put it into words; this knowledge just impresses itself on our awareness. The term comes from the fact that a gut feeling is literally a physiological response in our body, and this response is registered in the brain. In contrast to *knowing that*, gut-level knowledge is referred to as *knowing how*.

We know how someone else is feeling in the same way Lightman detects lies. If my wife is upset about something, she doesn't need to tell me or hold up a sign for me to figure it out. My right brain processes her micro expressions, tone of voice, and body posture in a matter of milliseconds, and produces an emotional response in me that carries information—or knowledge—within it. The same is true for you when you read others' emotions. You actually get a gut-level sensation in your body that has a certain meaning built into it—whether it's sadness, anger, or some other emotion. We actually catch others' feelings. This is how gut-level, or implicit, knowing works. Our brains process facial expressions, tone of voice, body posture, and all the subtle, nonverbal aspects of communication. And it's partly through implicit knowledge that we help others feel better when they feel bad; we catch each other's good feelings as well as bad.

IMPLICIT RELATIONAL KNOWLEDGE

The important subtype of implicit knowledge for our purposes is *implicit relational knowledge*. A client, Mark, demonstrated his implicit knowledge of emotionally significant relationships in a series of sessions with me. Mark was feeling upset about a work situation and he reached out to two close friends. He felt blown off and ultimately rejected by both friends over the course of a few weeks. He was devastated. These experiences of rejection reinforced his implicit relational knowledge that his need for support eventually overwhelmed others, leading them to withdraw from him.

Mark then shut down and withdrew from me and our work in therapy. He had come to expect at a gut level that I, too, would be overwhelmed by his needs for comfort and would abandon him. He wasn't consciously aware of this experience until we discussed it; however, he put into words his implicit relational knowledge when he told me, "Of course, you're consumed with your own life, and have no room for my needs." This is how he *knew* relationships worked—at least for him. And this implicit knowledge then influenced his expectations and ways of relating.

Mark knew in his head that this pattern doesn't necessarily happen with everyone. He also knew explicitly that I wasn't generally consumed with my own needs in our sessions, that I hadn't abandoned him in the past, and that it was unlikely that I would in the future. Mark had two conflicting sources of knowledge about how relationships work. So which one was right?

The answer is both, but in very different ways. Both aspects of knowledge are part of him in some sense, but when there is a disconnect between the two ways of knowing, our implicit relational knowledge wins out when it comes to how we relate to others. Although it may not be consistent with our explicit knowledge, our implicit knowledge reveals how we construct the meaning of our relational worlds. This is the starting point for any deep level of transformation. In short, *implicit relational knowledge is the foundational way of knowing in relationships*. It is this way of knowing that directly drives our capacity to love and how we relate to others. The reason is that this way of knowing is automatic and not under our direct control. As we'll see, explicit knowledge is important, but it must be integrated with implicit knowledge in order to affect our ability to love God and others. Our implicit knowledge of relationships also permeates our relationship with God, and sometimes it requires a deep search to truly grasp our real idea of God.

GOD IN OUR OWN IMAGE

When I told you Julia's story earlier, I mentioned an idea, often unspoken, but clearly present in our churches. It's the idea that our relationship with God is of a qualitatively different type than our human relationships. If this is the case, the thinking goes, then we should always feel close to God.

This mindset ignores our messy but very real relational knowledge of God. It boils down to an assumption that the ways of knowing that drive our human relationships somehow don't apply when it comes to our relationship with God.

In this view, there is a psychological part of us involved in our human relationships and a spiritual part that handles matters having to do with God and morality. This presents the possibility of a radical disconnect between our relationships with humans on the one hand, and with God on the other hand. This view, however, doesn't square with what the Bible has to say about love or the human soul, or with contemporary research on the association between our patterns of relationship with humans and with God.

First John makes it very clear that an intrinsic part of loving God is loving others:

> Dear friends, since God loved us that much, we surely ought to love each other. No one has ever seen God. But if we love each other, God lives in us, and his love is brought to full expression in us. . . . If someone says, "I love God," but hates a fellow believer, that person is a liar; for if we don't love people we can see, how can we love God, whom we cannot see? And he has given us this command: Those who love God must also love their fellow believers. (1 John 4:11-12; 20-21)

How we treat people reveals what is in our heart, and our heart doesn't magically change when it comes to our relationship with God. We have one heart out of which our relationships with God and humans flow.

The Bible also paints a picture of the human soul as being a unity. The Hebrew concept of the soul in the Old Testament is of a unified entity, not several different parts. The will, mind, emotions, and desires are unified and function as a whole—even if they're directed toward protecting yourself from emotional pain. Another place we see this is in the biblical concept of the heart in both the Old and New Testaments. The heart is described as the seat of wisdom,[9] volition, motives, desires (Exodus 35:5; Psalm 21:1-2; Acts 8:21-23; Romans 2:5 NIV), and emotions (e.g., sadness, 1 Samuel 1:8; joy, Proverbs 15:30; fear, Deuteronomy 28:65; uncertainty, John 14:1). In other words, all these different facets of our soul function together as a unified whole. What this means, then, is that there's not a separate part of us that relates to God. Our humanness infuses every aspect of our relationship with God. Spiritual growth involves becoming more fully human, not less.

In my work in psychotherapy, my experience has been that people's relational knowledge of God inevitably mirrors their relational knowledge of their attachment figures. In a very real sense, we create God in our own image. There isn't necessarily a one-to-one correspondence, but the parallels are typically striking. My experience resonates with a biblical picture of our souls as a psychospiritual unity.[10] From this perspective, it's not possible to separate relational processes from spiritual processes, or to separate psychological and spiritual domains of functioning. They are woven together in such a way that we can't neatly separate them. Just as our implicit relational knowledge drives how we actually relate to others in general, it also drives how we relate to God and our capacity to love. Our implicit relational knowledge is how we evaluate the meaning of any aspect of functioning, because it's automatic and not under our direct control.

I had been seeing Mark, mentioned above, in therapy for about two years when he began to withdraw from his relationship with God, and gradually pulled out of his spiritual community.[11] At first he was unaware of the meaning of this behavior, and he avoided discussing it with me. When we did process the issue, he felt extremely sad and became aware of a sense of abandonment by God. Mark's story of abandonment was being told indirectly, partly by his withdrawal from God and church. In other words, it was a gut-level experience of God that Mark hadn't put into words. Part of what contributed to Mark's implicit knowledge of God was years of experiences of his father being emotionally absent, and ultimately abandoning him in a way. We automatically carry our experiences with human attachment figures into our relationship with God.

As we talked more about his withdraw from his church, Mark experienced a stronger sense of abandonment by God. I suggested that this may be linked to the series of recent rejections he had experienced in close relationships, and ultimately to his experience of abandonment by his father. This resonated with him, and he was gradually able to put words to his gut-level experiences, further articulating the meaning of his sense of abandonment by God. As a result of this, Mark's implicit knowledge of God became clearer. This illustrates two key principles: (1) Mark's pattern of relationship with God was being driven by his implicit knowledge of God, not his explicit knowledge, and (2) his implicit knowledge of God mirrored his implicit knowledge of his human attachment figures. This works the same way in our relationship with God as it does in our human relationships. Implicit relational knowledge drives how we actually relate to and experience God.

We know more than we can say. We know some things in an intellectual way (explicit knowledge) and other things we know deep in our gut (implicit knowledge), such as knowing how to relate to others in a healthy, loving manner (implicit relational knowledge). Both forms of knowledge are important and play a role in spiritual and emotional growth. However, implicit relational knowledge directly drives how we relate to God and others. This relational way of knowing, then, is what ultimately needs to be transformed if we are to become more like Christ and find deep meaning in our lives. This type of knowledge is fundamentally shaped by emotion, the subject to which we now turn.

5

Once More *with* Feeling

THE SUMMER AFTER my sophomore year of college, I went back to the church I attended when I became a Christian. One Sunday in the college group the pastor talked about psychology and emotions. I don't remember his exact words, but he basically said you can't trust psychology, and you can't trust your emotions. Emotions, he contended, will lead you astray, so you need to focus on what the Bible says is true about you and your relationship with God. If you're depressed or anxious, don't allow those feelings any voice. Don't trust your emotions because they're unpredictable. Giving our emotions any credence, he argued, is like following a wild goose chase.

That was the first time I had ever heard this view stated overtly in an official church setting, but I recognized it as something that was often implied. This is a common view in many churches that is sometimes taught explicitly, but more often it's carried in the attitudes of church leaders. This was directly relevant to my life, so it stuck with me and forced me to evaluate what he was saying. Later, as I entered graduate school in psychology, started my own therapy, and began conducting therapy with clients, I had to grapple with this issue on many levels: How, I wondered, do emotions affect my spiritual growth and healing process? What role should emotions play in trying to help others heal and grow?

I've worked with many clients who also struggle with this message. Ken came to see me for his anxiety and depression. When he was in grade school, his mother had a "psychotic break"—she basically lost touch with reality and was in and out of hospitals for the rest of his growing up years. He often felt anxious and unsure about his salvation, and unworthy of God's love. Once he shared with a friend from church, and the friend told him to ignore his feelings and focus on his identity in Christ. Ken tried, but he couldn't make the anxiety and feelings of unworthiness go away.

So what do we do with this idea that we can't trust our emotions—that emotions simply lead us astray? Are emotions inferior to explicit knowledge? We have to start by recognizing that implicit, gut-level knowledge uses the language of emotions. Emotion is a fundamental way of knowing that is part of human nature. Does this mean that God created a system in the brain—a way of knowing—that can't be trusted?

I think the intent of the concern behind this message is valid, but it's not complete, and it's based on a misunderstanding that isn't informed by what we now know about emotion. Let's address the valid part first. Clearly, there are times when we "feel" like doing something that is overtly sinful. Clara, a Christian, came to see me for therapy because she was having an affair, and her husband found out and she wanted to save their marriage. She realized, at some level, that the affair wasn't worth the damage it was going to cause to her kids. But she was still having the affair during the early part of therapy. We could say that at one level Clara's emotions were driving her to pursue sexual intimacy outside of her marriage. Would we encourage Clara to "go with her feelings" in this sense? Aren't her feelings leading her astray? If we're talking about the pleasure Clara derived from the affair and her desire to continue it, then yes, Clara's feelings were leading her astray. Does this mean Clara should ignore all of her emotions and implicit knowledge and focus only on bolstering her explicit knowledge of God?

To answer this, we need a more robust understanding of emotion and how it works.

THE FEELING OF WHAT HAPPENS

What is the purpose of emotions? If they're just random misfirings that lead us astray, then it would seem they have no purpose. If we should ignore our emotions, as we sometimes hear in Christian circles, then emotions have no reason for existence. It turns out, however, that emotions have a very deep purpose that is integral to our well-being and spiritual growth.

Emotions are the basis of the implicit knowledge of relating in a healthy and loving way. Emotions are also inherently evaluative; they identify the subjective meaning of an event to us. Emotions tell us whether something is good or bad by making that thing feel good or bad (or somewhere on the spectrum from good to bad). They do this by producing changes in our internal organs in response to our experiences in the outside world. These physiological changes and characteristics create the overall feeling we have about our environment and ourselves. This is what neuroscientist Antonio Damasio calls "the feeling of what happens."[1]

A former client of mine, Frank, served in World War II and was a prisoner of war in Korea for four years. Many years later, he told me that when he would hear a sudden, loud noise like a car backfiring, he would respond with full-blown posttraumatic stress symptoms because, to him, the noise meant something different. Any noise remotely similar to a gunshot was encoded in the *fear* system in his brain, automatically alerting him to danger. When he experienced extreme anxiety and terror and the corresponding physiological changes from a noise like this, he was emotionally perceiving his subjective response to the noise, determined by the meaning assigned to it. And his brain had assigned this meaning based on past experiences in order to protect him.

Emotion, then, is the nonverbal and automatic way we evaluate the meaning of our experiences with respect to our well-being. Emotion also helps us know things in a different way than thinking does.

KNOWING THROUGH FEELING

When I was in the Army working as a psychologist, I dealt with a lot of clients who were suicidal.[2] Sometimes I would have to hospitalize them to keep them safe. I vividly remember one woman I evaluated. She was suicidal and had been hospitalized by one of the physicians, who turned the case over to me. After she had been in the hospital for a few days, they called me to evaluate whether she was ready to be discharged and begin outpatient psychotherapy. She assured me that her suicidal thoughts were fleeting, and that she had no intention of harming herself. After talking with her for about an hour, I decided to discharge her.

As I was walking from the hospital back to my office in a separate building, I noticed a nagging feeling of uneasiness growing in my gut. Something felt "off" about the whole situation, and I felt compelled to go check on her. *But why?* I asked myself. After all, I had just spent an hour interviewing this woman, and she flatly denied any active suicidal ideation, plan, or intent to harm herself. I had covered the bases. There was no apparent reason to go back and check on her. *She'll be fine*, I told myself. I tried to ignore the feeling as I kept walking back to my office.

But the nagging feeling just wouldn't go away. In fact, it grew stronger. What do you do in those moments when your gut seems to be telling you something, but you're not sure exactly what or why? Are your emotions and "nagging gut feelings" worthy of your attention? And what if they contradict the objective facts of the situation?

After walking a few more feet, I decided to go back and talk to the patient again. I turned around, went back to the hospital, and went straight to her room. She was still there, waiting for the discharge papers to be finalized. I sat down, looked her right in the eyes, and said in a gentle but direct tone, "Are you going to kill yourself?" She immediately burst into tears and admitted that she had lied to me, and that she was planning to kill herself as soon as she was discharged.

Somehow I had known that this woman was not okay, and what gave me this information was the feeling in my gut of what happened in our conversation. Emotions, then, carry information that is particularly vital for understanding people and loving others. Those nagging gut feelings do deserve your attention, but always with an evaluative eye. We now have a much greater understanding of how and why emotions pulse with implicit knowledge.

A fascinating study sheds some light on how I knew this patient was not okay. In a dramatic illustration of emotion as implicit relational knowledge, fifty-nine patients who had attempted suicide in the previous three days were interviewed by the same psychiatrist. The faces of the patients and psychiatrist were recorded during the interviews. One year later, ten of the fifty-nine patients made another suicide attempt (the "reattempter" group). The researchers tried to predict which patients would reattempt suicide using two types of information: the psychiatrist's predictions written immediately after the interviews, and the nonverbal communications (emotions) between the psychiatrist and patients. Which type of knowledge—explicit (written predictions) or implicit (emotions communicated through facial expressions)—would do the best job of predicting suicide reattempts?

It turned out that the psychiatrist's written predictions correctly identified reattempters in 29 percent of cases, whereas the analysis of emotions correctly classified reattempters in 81 percent of the cases.[3] That's a huge difference. In addition, the real predictive power came not from the *patients'* facial expression of emotion, but from the *psychiatrist's* facial expression of emotion. With patients who ended up reattempting suicide, the psychiatrist frowned more, showed more animated facial expressions, and exhibited a higher level of speech.

The researchers believe that the psychiatrist's negative expressions and increased facial activity were serving two purposes: regulating his own internal state and communicating with his patient. It appears that the patient created a synchronized emotional state in the psychiatrist, which in turn influenced his own nonverbal behavior. This is how the psychiatrist "knew" that a particular patient would reattempt. He didn't know this in words (explicit knowledge), but he knew this in his body, facial expressions, and emotions—literally in his gut.

A famous case of a stroke survivor reveals another angle on how emotion carries information. "Patient X," as doctors call him, suffered two strokes that severed the connections between his eyes and the rest of the visual system in his visual cortex. His eyes could take in signals, but his brain didn't know the signals were there and couldn't decode them. It seemed Patient X was completely blind. When he was shown shapes or photos, he had no idea what was in front of him. But when he was shown pictures of people expressing emotion, like an angry face, he was able to guess the emotion on the face at a rate far better than chance. How is this possible?

Brain scans conducted while Patient X was guessing the emotions showed that his brain used a different pathway than the normal pathway for seeing. Normally, visual input travels from the eyes to the thalamus, which processes sensory data, and then to the visual cortex. In Patient X's case, his brain sent information from the thalamus straight to the amygdala, which computes the *emotional meaning* of a nonverbal message. So Patient X was *feeling* the emotion on the faces that he couldn't see—a condition known as "affective blindsight."[4] He "knew" the emotions on the faces through his own emotions, not through conscious, verbal knowledge. Just as we know things through feelings, we also feel ideas through stories, which is a form of implicit knowledge.

STORY: FEELING AN IDEA

In 1977, when I was in grade school, my dad took me to see the first Star Wars movie, *Episode IV: A New Hope*.[5] I remember the anticipation. I had been collecting stickers in a Star Wars sticker book before I saw the movie and understood what it was all about. I knew it was a big story; I just didn't know *how* big. Then one sunny day in Southern California, we waited in a very long line, and my mind was blown by the biggest movie I'd ever seen. It was like nothing I'd ever experienced. Star Wars managed to combine vast galaxies, cool starships like the Millennium Falcon, and the intimate personal struggles of Luke Skywalker—all played out in an epic battle of good versus evil. This timeless story, of course, went on to become one of the most popular movie series of all time, bridging a generation with the recent release of *The Force Awakens*.

Part of the reason Star Wars has captured the hearts of generations is that it follows a classic story structure that provides clarity, helps us make sense of our experience, and draws us toward something transcendent. Story shapes our vision of reality. It nourishes our soul in a way that intellectual understanding never could. Why else do we go to the movies and sit in the dark with mostly strangers for two hours, our eyes glued to the screen with rapt attention? When you stop and think about it, it's pretty strange. Have you ever seen this happen at a lecture? On rare occasions, an extraordinary lecturer may hold the rapt attention of an audience more than a few minutes. If this does happen, the speaker is likely using story to capture the audience's attention.

The fact that we give ourselves so fully to share an experience with a group of strangers in a theater speaks to the power of story. Story draws us in through implicit knowledge embedded within its very structure.

In life, the meaning of our experiences doesn't make itself known in real time. Aristotle observed this in his study of story: Why, he asked, do we react to an event in real life one way, but when we encounter the same event in story, we react another way?[6] The reason is that in life, ideas and their emotional meaning emerge separately.

When my son Aiden was fifteen years old he broke his leg playing soccer. When I saw the look on his face when he went down, I experienced a rush of adrenaline as I ran out to him thinking, *Oh no! Is he okay?* For the rest of the evening, my focus wasn't on the meaning of the event in the grand scheme of my life. Instead I was anxiously focused on getting my son to the ER to diagnose the injury and get him the care he needed. Only later, in the coolness of time, was I able to reflect on the meaning of my son's injury. Our bodies, I was reminded, don't always work the way they're intended—sometimes due to illness, other times due to injury. In the midst of caring for my son over the next few days, however, a deeper bond was forged. I learned anew that we become more deeply connected when we suffer with others. The deeper bonds that can grow when we suffer with others can help us become more like Christ, as we learn to seek the good of others. We understand the meaning our experiences, such as my son's broken leg, only with reflection in time.

Whereas life brings meaning and emotion separately, story unites them with *aesthetic emotion*.[7] In his landmark book *Story*, screenwriter Robert McKee tells us "the exchange between artist and audience expresses idea directly through the senses and perceptions, intuition and emotion."[8] Story doesn't explain its view of life—its knowledge—in abstract ideas. Instead it creates aesthetic emotion— the feeling of an idea. This is implicit knowledge—a knowing that comes from your emotions and experience. Stories carry knowledge within them, housed in the very structure of the sequence of events and the experiences we live through vicariously. Regardless of genre, the meaning of a story is expressed or dramatized in the emotionally charged climax of the story. The hero comes to a moment of decisive choice—a true dilemma—at the story's climax. This is called the "obligatory scene."

In the climactic scene of *The Return of the Jedi*, Luke Skywalker takes on his father, Darth Vader, in a light saber duel. The evil Emperor is watching, provoking Luke to give in to his anger. He knows that if Luke does it will move him toward the dark side of the Force. At one point in the battle, Luke flies into a rage and gets the upper hand, cutting off Vader's hand. He gave into his anger for a moment and experienced its power and consequences. The Emperor goads Luke to take his father's place as his servant—to give in to his anger and the dark side of the Force. In that moment, Luke had a decisive choice to make: kill Vader or resist his anger.

Movies communicate ideas directly through the medium of visual story. You see an idea played out in the structure of the events that occur. More specifically, you *feel the idea*. It's a deeper and more direct form of knowledge than grasping a proposition. When Luke chooses to throw down his light saber, refusing to kill Darth Vader, you immediately feel the controlling idea of Star Wars: good prevails over evil when we resist our dark side and trust in the greater good of humanity (the Force).

Stories communicate implicit knowledge in the same way children internalize morality from their attachment figures. We see the values and morality of our attachment figures played out before us in how they live their lives. We see our dad put someone else's interests above his own, even when it's hard, and our heart tells us: *That is how I ought to live because I want be like my dad and I want his approval.* Likewise, when we see ourselves in a story's hero, it helps us create meaning as we reflect on the story of our own lives. We're drawn into Star Wars because we identify with Luke Skywalker. We sense our shared humanity, struggles, and self-doubt. We see the truth of our own struggles in a new light. Does Luke have what it takes to become a Jedi, resist his own dark side, and defeat the evil Empire? With Luke, we ask ourselves: Do I have the internal fortitude to resist my dark side and face the challenges currently before me? Luke doesn't turn to Han Solo at the end of the movie and say, "Hey, you know what Han? I've realized through this adventure that when we resist our dark side and trust in the Force, only then will good prevail over evil." No. Instead, we see this idea dramatized in action, and we feel it in our bones as our heart tells us: *That is how I ought to live because I want be like Luke.*

The knowledge we gain from story is implicit—*the feeling of an idea.* Sometimes this idea focuses on the global societal level: good versus evil in *Star Wars*. Sometimes the controlling idea speaks more directly to the relational and psychological levels of our lives. Here we feel an idea about how relationships affect the human psyche, including our own.

In *Good Will Hunting*, as we learn about Will's traumatic background and witness him push away those closest to him, we feel the idea of the negative human experience being communicated: trauma damages our sense of self, and profoundly hinders our ability to love. Then, in the park scene, Sean confronts Will and invites him into a process of vulnerability, connection, and healing. Will is faced with a choice: continue pushing away his emotional pain and the people in his life, or face his fears and open up. When Will walks back into Sean's office for his next appointment, and begins to sob when Sean compassionately repeats, "It's not your fault," we feel the psychological controlling idea: healing begins when we allow others to bear witness to our pain.

As in story, the knowledge we gain from relationships in real life is implicit—the subjective truth of how relationships work for us based on our unique relational experiences. This knowledge guides our lives, mostly without our conscious awareness. There are things we know deep in our soul that we have never thought—*unthought knowns*.[9] While we may not have consciously thought the things we know *implicitly* in our emotions and relationships, they are real nonetheless. This way of knowing also drives how we make decisions.

FEELING OUR WAY TO GOOD DECISIONS

During my senior year of college, I had to make a big decision about where to go to graduate school for clinical psychology. My girlfriend at the time, Liz (now my wife), and I had both been accepted to the clinical psychology program at Rosemead School of Psychology where we were attending college. We were also both accepted to several other graduate programs. We had been dating about six months; long enough that our relationship felt like it was "going somewhere," but not long enough that we were talking about getting married. It was an awkward time to have to make this decision. Did I want to want to attend the same graduate program as my (then) girlfriend for five or six years? What if we broke up in the middle of the program? Being stuck together in classes for several years would be all kinds of awkward. But the other option of attending different programs had risks as well. What if we drifted apart trying to manage a long-distance relationship?

How was I to make this decision—just go with my gut, or analyze my way to the most rational choice? Shortly before this, I had heard the college pastor I mentioned above talk about emotions and psychology. He not only taught that we shouldn't give any credence to painful emotions, he also told us that we shouldn't rely on emotions in making decisions. Emotions, he contended, can lead us astray in our decisions. As a college student, I had an uneasy feeling about this teaching, but I wasn't quite sure why.

At some time in your life, you've probably been told, or at least heard, that you should "keep your emotions out of it." The idea here is that in order to make rational (which is code for "good") decisions, you need to set your emotions aside and make decisions based purely on rational factors. This, supposedly, is what mature people do.

Since I was going into the field of psychology, I felt compelled to sort this issue out in my mind. But now I needed to not just sort it out in theory, I needed to apply these principles to a very big decision in my life. Even though I felt uneasy about that pastor's teaching, I had heard this view enough that I had internalized it. The intellectual approach to spiritual growth trickled down into my decision-making. Whether I was making decisions about a job or a relationship, I often tried to rationally analyze the options to arrive at the best choice. Likewise, in this case I tried to analyze the pros and cons of attending various programs. I talked with Liz about the pros and cons of attending the same program versus different programs, and about making the decision separately versus together. I tried not to let my feelings influence the process or the decision, even though I wasn't sure exactly what that meant. I made a list of the positive factors and risk factors, hoping the rational decision would jump off the page at me.

At the end of the day, I felt paralyzed. I couldn't make a decision. How do you rationally compare a close romantic relationship to a psychology program? Comparing the pros and cons felt like comparing apples and oranges.

In retrospect, when I tried to make decisions this way, I often ended up feeling confused and stuck. I think we all experience some degree of confusion and paralysis when we try to set aside our emotions in decision-making. I've worked with many clients who have struggled with this. They shut down their emotions at the cost of good decisions. Why does this happen? And how, then, do we make good decisions that promote our own and others' well-being?

EMOTIONS AS THE GATEKEEPER TO DECISIONS

We've learned that it's impossible to fully set our emotions aside when we make decisions and, perhaps more importantly, that we shouldn't do this. Emotions are what drive and motivate our decisions below conscious awareness. In fact, people with damage to their emotion systems make very poor decisions. This is because emotions carry a certain kind of information, implicit knowledge, to which our conscious rational thinking doesn't have access.

Leading neuroscientist Antonio Damasio developed the Somatic-Marker Hypothesis, which helps us understand how emotions undergird decision-making.[10] More research is needed, but the contours of the emotion-based decision-making process are becoming clearer. When we make a decision, various possibilities flash through our mind subconsciously. The body responds to each possibility with an emotional tag, which generates a gut feeling. These are neural cues, which connect an event (or an imagined event in consideration) to a bodily state—pleasant or unpleasant. This produces urges or "action tendencies" to behave in ways that our subconscious mind believes to be aligned with our best interest. Sometimes these feelings emerge in our conscious awareness, but sometimes they don't. At some level, however, this process focuses our attention toward certain outcomes and away from others. Damasio refers to these tags as *somatic markers* because they take place in the body (*soma*) and they leave a mark.

For example, let's say you and your friend are trying to decide what to do tonight. Among the reasonable options being bandied about (e.g., go to dinner, see a movie) your friend suggests you go dancing. As you consider this option, you immediately get a very bad gut feeling as you have visions of people laughing at you doing the junior high two-step in the seventh grade. You really do not want to repeat this experience. Your mind almost immediately shuts this down as a viable option because of the bad feeling. After the emotional tagging takes place, you will then construct rational arguments for why you shouldn't do it (e.g., it's too far; you have a strained hamstring, etc.).

Somatic markers narrow down the pool of live choices. Negative markers function as a warning or alarm signal for potentially bad choices. Conversely, positive markers provide a neurological floodlight or incentive for potentially good choices. In doing this, somatic markers provide immediate direction and motivation. In other words, emotional signals propel you in a direction (to do something or to *not* do something) without making the reasons clear.[11] Rational analysis can still be helpful, but it comes online only after the possibilities have been filtered by emotional tagging. Emotions, then, play a gatekeeper role in thinking. By the time you rationally think through things, your somatic-marker system has already biased you toward certain options and away from other options. This process undergirds the vast majority of conflict. If we truly understood and embraced the unwitting ways our emotions bias our thoughts, it would radically decrease the conflict in our lives and promote true empathy.

People with no somatic markers are left adrift with no motivation to move in one direction versus another. Without the ability to emotionally sense the consequences of various actions, their rational analysis does them no good, and they end up either paralyzed or acting on the basis of their immediate impulses. Speaking of those who lack the capacity for somatic marking, Damasio states, "It is emotion that allows you to mark things as good, bad, or indifferent, literally in the flesh. And it is that kind of emotional impetus they are lacking. They cannot conjure up . . . an emotional state that would [cause them to] decide . . . in one direction or another."[12]

So how did somatic markers play out in my decision about which psychology graduate program to attend? As the deadline for graduate school decisions approached, I knew I had to find a way to get past my paralysis. I met with a close mentor to get his input. After talking for a few minutes, he asked me, "All things considered, what does your gut tell you? What do you want to do?"

The answer in my mind was immediate: I wanted to attend Rosemead with Liz. I knew deep down that our relationship, even at that stage, was more important than the particular program I attended. My emotion system stamped a value (or a somatic marker) on this decision that occurred outside of my conscious rational processing. It created a positive gut feeling associated with the outcome of attending graduate school with Liz, and a negative gut feeling associated with being separated at different programs. It incentivized and motivated me to make the choice to attend graduate school with Liz (so far as it was within my control). I told Liz how I felt, and she felt the same way; we had both arrived at the same decision. We attended Rosemead, a good decision with a happy ending—we got married after our first year of graduate school and never had to sit awkwardly through classes together after breaking up!

Where does this leave us with emotions and decision-making? First, don't try to set aside your emotions when making a decision. You can't do that anyway! Your brain tags events based on emotion before you can rationally think things through. But that doesn't mean you never think things through and just go with your feelings. Instead, you want to tune into your feelings about choices you're considering and give yourself some time and space (if possible) to allow your somatic markers to reorganize based on your thought processes. In this way, you're using implicit and explicit knowledge. We'll come back to this later when we talk about the knowledge spiral. In addition to reorganizing based on rational thought, we also need to evaluate and train our emotions (and somatic markers).

Why? Like every other aspect of human functioning, our emotion-based evaluation and motivation system is fallen. It doesn't always line up with God's design. Let's return to the case of Clara.

EMOTION AND GOD'S DESIGN

We are created to find meaning in loving relational connection with God and others—this is essential to human nature. When we work outside of God's design for connection, we don't find meaning or fulfillment.

Clara, my client who was engaged in an affair, felt very alone in her marriage. The meaning tagged to her experience of the affair was that it was a connection of some type. But it was an unhealthy form of connection according to God's design. The meaning our brains tag to events is not always consistent with the way God designed us to connect. Because of our unhealthy relational experiences (which we certainly contribute to), our brains and souls can develop such that they tag these familiar unhealthy experiences with the meaning of "connection." So, in this case, Clara's soul had become dysfunctional to the point that her brain tagged an illicit sexual relationship with the meaning of connection, but it was a substitute for real connection the way God designed it.

What, then, is the role of emotion in regard to helping Clara? Because emotion is the meaning Clara tags to the affair at a gut level, it's the entry point into her heart and her heart is what ultimately needs to be transformed. Some might counsel Clara to ignore her feelings and stop the affair. Stopping the affair is clearly the right thing to do, but ignoring her feelings will not lead to lasting, heart-level change in how she actually relates to God and others. Her emotions need to be experienced, processed, and transformed in the context of healthy relationships.

Emotions are an intrinsic aspect of implicit relational knowledge. As such, they have a deep purpose. Emotions are the way our minds evaluate the subjective meaning of events. They contain implicit knowledge—a certain kind of information that is critical for us to grow and heal. Ultimately, however, we don't grow by simply "going with our feelings." We always have to compare the meaning our gut-level system assigns to an event against God's Word and design for us. One crucial role of explicit knowledge of God and his Word is that it provides the standard for evaluating the implicit meanings revealed in our emotions. Sometimes our implicit knowledge and goals match up with God's design for us, but sometimes they don't. If we ignore our emotions, however, we'll never find the "You are here" dot on the map of our heart. And if we don't know where our heart is, we can't guide it in the right direction.

If we want to be transformed at the very core of our being, the meanings revealed in our emotional responses must be the starting point. We have to start where our heart is—our emotion-based tags—because that's what God wants to transform, and that is the place from which love flows. There is no way to bypass the "You are here" of our heart. We must start with our implicit relational knowledge. This relational knowledge is the very foundation of the next topic in our journey together—attachment bonds that shape our soul and ability to love.

PART THREE

ATTACHMENT
BONDS

6

Born *to* Connect

JOHN BOWLBY, A PSYCHIATRIST and the founder of *attachment theory*, was on a mission. As a child Bowlby saw his mother for about an hour a day and was raised primarily by a "nursemaid," which was typical for upper-middle class British homes in the early twentieth century. Minnie was a warm, nurturing mother figure and Bowlby became very attached to her. When he was nearly four years old, Nursemaid Minnie left the family. Following Minnie's departure, Bowlby was cared for by Nanny Friend—a decidedly less-nurturing woman. The young Bowlby was, of course, devastated, and he later described this as a tragic loss. This early loss of a mother figure set him on a trajectory toward studying the effects of losing a close, maternal figure.

After completing his adult psychiatric training, Bowlby took a position in 1936 at the London Child Guidance Clinic. Based on his time there, as well as his own experience, Bowlby came to believe that maternal separation had devastating and long-lasting effects on children. Bowlby's idea contradicted the predominant views of his day. The typical view of psychoanalysts and mental health professionals was that children don't need a warm, nurturing connection with their parents. According to the conventional wisdom, separation and loss didn't cause problems. The problems they were seeing in children in the clinics were attributed to unconscious drives and internal fantasies—wishful thinking that needed to be set straight by accepting the harsh realities of life.

Setting out to prove his theory, Bowlby investigated the history of forty-four juvenile thieves.[1] He found that a higher proportion of thieves than clinic children had experienced a prolonged separation from their mothers. More specifically, seventeen of forty-four thieves had experienced early and prolonged maternal separation (six months or longer) compared to only two of the comparison group who had no history of stealing. In his paper, Bowlby coined the term "affectionless psychopath" to describe juvenile thieves who demonstrated a lack of concern for others, presumably due to the lack of warm and consistent care. These findings drew attention to the importance of children's early relational experiences with parents.

In 1950, the World Health Organization (WHO) was looking for an expert to report on the mental health status of homeless children after World War II, and Bowlby's work and research background made him the obvious choice.[2] He traveled throughout Europe and the United States, meeting with the leading experts in child development, and conducted an extensive literature review on the topic. Based on this work, he published the monograph *Maternal Care and Mental Health* in 1951.[3] He later published a popular version, *Child Care and the Growth of Love*,[4] which became an instant bestseller. Bowlby concluded that children who had experienced severe deprivation of maternal care typically developed very similar symptoms as the affectionless thieves.

Armed with his WHO experiences, Bowlby started his own research unit in order to systematically study the effects of separation on the personality development of young children. He recruited James Robertson, who had worked in Anna Freud's Hampstead residential children's nursery. Anna Freud was Sigmund Freud's daughter, a prominent psychoanalytic theorist in her own right. Together they observed children in foundling homes where orphaned and displaced children resided, sometimes for long periods of time. They were shocked by what they saw. In fact, Robertson was so disturbed after two years of observing these young children in distress that he decided he had to do something to help. With Bowlby's support and a shoestring budget, he made the landmark film *A Two-Year-Old Goes to Hospital*,[5] which documented the intense emotional suffering of a young child separated from her mother.

Let's travel back to a British foundling home in 1947 and witness what Bowlby and Robertson would have observed. The hallways of the institution are busy with the hustle and bustle of nurses and staff as they attend to the children placed in their care. There is a large room, full of young children, mostly under the age of three. Cribs and beds line the walls of the room, and toys are scattered throughout. A twelve-month-old boy sits in the corner staring into space, rocking back and forth rhythmically. A two-year-old girl on the other side of the room is crying loudly, but intermittently. Just when you think she has calmed down, she bursts into tears again, startling you. Several other children are playing quietly on the floor, each in their own private world. Another has just watched his parents leave, and he is screaming as he pounds on the door with his fists. You then notice a little girl in a crib and walk over to her. She stares straight ahead with a blank, yet desperate stare. The look on her face tells you she wants to cry, yet she is beyond the hope that brings tears. She has not seen her parents for an entire year.[6]

The children who survived all experienced severe loss. They went through three clear stages of grief that Bowlby documented.[7] First, they *protested* loudly, desperately, and angrily, demanding that their parents return. After a period of time, they transitioned into *despair*. A look of desperate longing was written on their faces, as the hope that their mothers would ever return slipped out of reach. At some point, when all hope of seeing their mothers again seemed to have disappeared, the children became *detached* from human connection.

At first, the staff thought this was a good sign, because the children became more sociable and seemed happier—at least on the surface. Things were more pleasant on the wards. But when their parents did eventually return, the children treated them as complete strangers, only interested in the things their parents brought them. They would run up to their parents to get candy, and then turn away as if they didn't know their parents. It became clear that something was very wrong with these children. It was like an internal switch for connection had been turned off. They had lost the ability to form close relationships, and this would cause profound difficulties throughout their lives. Many parents became exasperated that, years later, their children still had difficulty expressing affection toward them. Something in their souls had been seriously damaged.

As if that weren't tragic enough, 10 to 20 percent of these children died—even in the best foundling homes. When the staff had to put something down for cause of death on the death certificates, they weren't sure what to write at first. These children weren't dying from malnourishment. They had food, clothing, and shelter. What, then, was the cause of death? Eventually they settled on "failure to thrive"— a phrase coined by psychoanalyst René Spitz, who worked extensively with orphans. This phenomenon was captured poignantly by an eighteenth-century Spanish bishop: "In the orphanage the child becomes sad, and many of them die of sadness."[8] This, tragically, was the typical scenario in foundling homes in Britain and North America in the 1940s and 1950s.

How did these children lose the capacity for human connection? How is it that many of them withered away and died, even though their physical needs were met? The answer is that these children were not spoken for. There was no one to consistently care for them; no specific person they could turn to for comfort. These children's physical needs were met, but their needs for relational connection and attachment were not. What caused things to go drastically wrong is that nurses weren't assigned to take care of individual children, so the children weren't able to develop a stable attachment to any specific caregiver. They had lost the most important person in their lives—their primary attachment figure.[9]

These tragedies raise the flip side of this question. What did these children need in order to prevent this, to flourish spiritually, to find meaning in life, and to thrive? In the first part of *Maternal Care and Mental Health*, Bowlby summarizes what children need: "What is believed to be essential for mental health is that the infant and young child should experience a warm, intimate and continuous relationship with his mother (or permanent mother-substitute) in which both find satisfaction and enjoyment."[10] This can also be with a father or father-substitute—Bowlby's work was based on research conducted in the mid-twentieth century when it was more common for mothers to play the role of primary attachment figure. With cultural shifts toward more involvement of fathers, and subsequent research on the father's role as an attachment figure, it is now generally understood that the necessary "warm, intimate and continuous relationship" can indeed be fulfilled by fathers as well.

If failure to thrive was caused by lack of connection, then it stands to reason that we need human connection in order to thrive. We all need close emotional connection and, more specifically, secure attachment relationships. Our need to connect is deeper than we realize as we go through the hustle and bustle of our day-to-day lives. Our emotional and spiritual well-being depend on it. Without connection and secure attachment, a sense of meaning and purpose will elude us. We're born to connect—prewired to form a specific kind of deep connection called an attachment bond.

THE POWER OF HUMAN CONNECTION

More than two million people in the United States have been diagnosed with schizophrenia. Because it's believed to have a strong genetic component, the standard treatment for many years has been strong doses of antipsychotic medications that reduce hallucinations and delusions, but often cause debilitating side effects like tremors and weight gain. The predominant thinking, until recently, has been that genes are the main culprit in this disorder, so relationships and "talk therapy" don't really help schizophrenia. This thinking is changing as we learn more about the power of relational connection.

Tim, the brother of a friend of mine, was diagnosed with schizophrenia in his early adulthood. Like many people diagnosed with schizophrenia, he had his first "psychotic break" in his early 20s. Tim didn't receive much treatment for the first few years, and at one point made a serious suicide attempt. He spent the next several years going on and off antipsychotic medications while being in and out of psychiatric hospitals. The medication helped, but the environment in the psychiatric hospitals wasn't conducive to healing—to say the least. He continued to struggle with various symptoms, including hearing voices. He couldn't work or maintain meaningful relationships. For numerous years, Tim trudged through life scared and lonely. Then things started to change.

Ned, a retired pastor, and his wife, Jean, invited Tim to live with them on their ranch. Tim accepted their offer and lived with them for almost a year. Ned and Jean were both joyful and nurturing people. They listened to Tim and loved him. He spent time in nature and went on hikes with Ned. They encouraged him and helped him to begin rebuilding his life while also giving him the space he needed to heal. They provided a structured life for Tim, but most importantly, they saw past his diagnosis and connected with the person behind it.

Shortly after this period, Tim began working for his brother, David, in his ceramics business. David, also very nurturing, gave Tim the flexibility to work when he could and take time off when he needed it. Although he started off slowly, Tim ended up managing some aspects of the business seven years later. This was a huge part of Tim's recovery and healing. It gave him a sense of purpose and meaning. Tim also later received counseling. His counselor listened and empathized with his experience. In particular, he helped Tim gain direction for his career, which later led to a positive tipping point.

Over a period of time, Tim gradually got better. As he felt understood and experienced a deep connection with Ned and Jean, his symptoms improved significantly and he became more connected to a community. He went on to get a college degree in land surveying and got a job in his field. This gave him a newfound sense of confidence. Tim now has a good job that he finds meaningful. A few years ago, he met a woman and fell in love. He's developed a healthy relationship with her, and they recently got engaged. He still has struggles, to be sure, but Tim is now functioning well and has a fulfilling life because people reached into his darkness and connected with him. Loving connection, it turns out, has the power to overcome genetic vulnerabilities, because we are born to connect.

Tim's story illustrates that we are profoundly relational beings. The absence of close relationships is a health risk factor that plays a larger role than smoking, obesity, and physical activity in its effects on mortality rates.[11] Close relationships help us cope with stress and meet our need for social connection. In addition, social connection is foundational for physical and mental health, and for meaning and spiritual growth into the likeness of Christ. This is evident in Tim's story, as loneliness made his mental illness worse and made it more difficult to cope with stress. In contrast, as Tim developed close relationships and felt more connected, his emotional and spiritual well-being improved.

The scientific evidence suggesting that God created us to connect is mounting. Because we are so deeply prewired to connect, the health and vitality of our connections greatly affect all aspects of our well-being, including our spiritual well-being. Our closest relationships affect us for good or for ill—there is no escaping the impact. However, the good news is that understanding our relational nature can help us pursue the connections with God and others that we need to heal and grow and find meaning in our lives. One place we see the evidence that we're prewired to connect is research suggesting that relational connections in general, and attachment relationships in particular, shape the expression of genes.

ATTACHMENT AND GENES

Until recently, mental health practitioners and scientists thought schizophrenia was caused mainly by one's genetic makeup. But Tim's story challenges this idea and highlights the debate about the role of genes versus environmental factors in our development. Tim didn't make sufficient progress in his mental health with the conventional treatments and medications. However, loving relationships had a profound healing impact over time.

What should we make of this? Was this a fluke? An outlier? Are our health, well-being, and sense of meaning really determined by our ticket in the genetic lottery? Thankfully, Tim's story is not an outlier. Though genetics and medication certainly play a role, they are not the only factors that contribute to our well-being. Connection is also a major factor because we are born to connect.

Recent research is shedding more light on Tim's story. A group of researchers set out to test a new treatment program for schizophrenia that challenges the old thinking and is based on the idea that connection heals. In evaluating an early treatment program called "NIMH RAISE," these researchers compared a comprehensive treatment approach to first-episode psychosis that emphasized relational connection (i.e., talk therapy and family support) to a typical community care approach that emphasized medication.[12] Results showed that the comprehensive relational approach, as a whole, led to better outcomes. Participants in this program: (1) stayed in treatment longer; (2) experienced greater improvement in quality of life and symptoms; and (3) had higher levels of involvement in work and school. This is just one area beginning to show the power of connection to overcome genetic vulnerabilities.

We've also learned from anxious monkeys that the way in which genes affect behavioral outcomes depends on the quality of our relationships. One study found that about 15 to 20 percent of rhesus monkeys seemed to carry a heritable trait of anxiety. In situations most monkeys would experience as novel and interesting, these monkeys became very anxious. In addition, they produced significantly higher levels of a stress hormone called cortisol. However, when these anxious monkeys who are genetically at risk were placed under the care of highly nurturing female monkeys, their anxiety disappeared! The improved social environment seems to have buffered or removed the genetic vulnerability to anxiety.[13]

Because of research like this, scientists are rethinking the so-called nature-nurture debate. A familiar discussion, one view holds that *nature*, or our genetic makeup, largely determines how our brains develop and consequently how every aspect of our personhood develops. The other view, *nurture*, holds that our life experiences play the major role in determining who we become. Over the past few decades, this debate has completely imploded. Contemporary scientists consider this dichotomy an unhelpful way to think about development. The Commission on Children at Risk states: "The old 'nature versus nurture' debate—focusing on whether heredity or environment is the main determinant of human conduct—is no longer relevant to serious discussions of child well-being and youth programming."[14] Part of the reason is that relational connections affect the brain circuits that process emotions, meaning, and relationships. This means we can't neatly separate nature from nurture like we once thought we could.

There is now convincing scientific evidence that our development results from the *interaction* of experience and our unfolding genetic potential, which sheds more light on our relational nature.[15] Genes have two main functions: (1) they provide a filter for information that is to be passed down to the next generation, and (2) they have a "transcription" function that determines when genes are expressed through the process of protein synthesis, based on the information encoded within their DNA. It turns out that transcription is directly influenced by relational experiences, which means relationships influence how neurons connect to form the circuits that make up our brains. Relational connections influence the formation of new synaptic connections in the brain, changes in the strength of neural connections, and the dissolution of neural connections.[16]

The *Hardwired to Connect* report by the Commission on Children at Risk explains this concept using a helpful analogy. If you think of genes as an alphabet from which "words" are produced that represent the biochemical messengers of our nervous system, relational experiences influence *which* letters are transcribed, *how often* they are transcribed, and in *what order* they are transcribed, all of which determine the content of the biochemical messages in our nervous system.[17] In other words, relational connections influence the way our genes are expressed, and the expression of our genes in turn changes the neural networks in our brains. The physical structure of neural networks is how our brains record or remember information. Attachment relationships shape not only our genetic expression, but our sense of self and how we relate to others.

We're born to connect. We grieve when connection is lost, and even infants show clear signs of the grieving process when they're separated from their attachment figures. Some infants who have lost this most fundamental attachment relationship even die—a phenomenon that came to be known as "failure to thrive." Attachment bonds, and relational connection more generally, play a vital role—in interaction with genes—in our development and healing. Evidence is emerging to suggest that relational connection can go a long way in healing disorders, such as schizophrenia, that were once thought to be genetically determined.

Human connection, then, is foundational for our overall well-being in all areas of life, including spirituality and a sense of meaning in life. We turn next to the process of how we become attached.

7

Becoming Attached

JAKE CAME TO SEE ME when his on-again, off-again relationship with his girlfriend had maxed out his anxiety. He was constantly anxious—worried that his girlfriend would leave him, or that she wouldn't be there to comfort him when he needed it. His anxiety was crippling his life. He couldn't concentrate at work and he was starting to have panic attacks. He felt sad much of the time.

Jake needed someone to help him process his painful feelings and provide emotional support during this trying time. We met once a week and talked about his relationship with his girlfriend and his anxieties and fears. I tried to empathize with his feelings and help him feel that they were understandable. We worked together on managing his overwhelming feelings of anxiety and loss.

As we got deeper into therapy, though, it became clear that this was not enough. Coping strategies weren't sufficient. Jake needed something more. He needed an attachment bond with a caregiver to rebuild his internal sense of security.

Jake is not alone. It turns out that we all need attachment relationships to grow and heal.

THE NATURE OF ATTACHMENT

There is strong scientific evidence that human beings are born to form attachment relationships; that we are "born to connect." You can think of this as our "relational hardware." Here is how Allan Schore, a neuropsychologist and leading thinker in this area, puts it: "The idea is that we are born to form attachments, that our brains are physically wired to develop in tandem with another's, through emotional communication, beginning before words are spoken."[1] The *Hardwired to Connect* report, developed by the American Institute of Values, formulates the idea this way: "The mechanisms by which we become and stay attached to others are biologically primed and increasingly discernable in the basic structure of the brain."[2]

There are two aspects of attachment: the attachment system and an attachment relationship. In the broadest sense, the attachment system is an innate (prewired) system that influences and organizes motivational, emotional, and memory processes with emotionally significant people, or "attachment figures."

An attachment relationship is a particular kind of relationship—a deep connection between an attachment figure, such as a parent or caregiver, and someone on the receiving end of that care, such as a child. When a child becomes attached to her parent, usually by six months of age, something happens inside of each one and between the two of them. An invisible bond develops that is supported by a literal brain-to-brain linkup between parent and child. The way this invisible bond shows itself, attachment researchers tell us, is through three characteristics.

First, infants seek to stay physically close to their attachment figure, and—the flip side of this coin—they become distressed when separated from their attachment figure. (There is typically a primary attachment figure, but often times there are multiple attachment figures.) Infants regulate connection by being physically close to their attachment figure. However, as we grow, emotional connection relies less on physical proximity and more on the memory of the felt presence of the attachment figure. Second, attachment figures provide—to varying degrees—a *haven of safety* in times of distress, and third, a *secure base* from which to explore the world. Overall, when they are comforting and empathic, attachment figures provide children a sense of felt security about themselves and their worlds. Our sense of felt security comes primarily from the specific people to whom we are attached.

If you're a parent or have seen children with their parents, you know what this experience is like. When young children get hurt physically or emotionally, they don't run to any random adult for comfort. They run to Mommy or Daddy or some other attachment figure; no one else will do. Adults aren't interchangeable when it comes to providing comfort. To be attached means that you are "spoken for" by your attachment figure(s). It means someone in this world has signed up to look out for you—to always be *for* you. Thankfully, I experienced this with my dad. I always felt my dad believed in me and was for me, which provided a secure base and haven of safety. I knew I could go to him if I was hurt or upset, and he would comfort me.

I've referred here mostly to childhood, but attachment impacts us throughout our entire lives. As adults, we continue to form attachment relationships with others. However the way we connect on an emotional level shifts from physical closeness in infancy, to emotional intimacy or "felt security" in adulthood.

In addition to parental figures, we become attached to spouses, close friends, and to God. If we have close contact with a supervisor, we can become attached in a certain sense because our boss is an authority figure. Even if we don't become emotionally attached to a boss, research suggests that we become symbolically attached to leaders and organizations because of what they represent. Because of this, attachment plays a powerful—and often unseen—role in how we follow and lead.

Neuroscience has taught us that the physical brain structures that process our relational experiences (e.g., the orbital frontal cortex, located between the cortex and subcortex) are *dependent* on relational experiences with attachment figures in order to grow and develop in a healthy manner. Neuroscientists refer to this characteristic as "experience-dependent." For example, when a mother and baby gaze at each other, or engage in "protoconversation," it stimulates the growth of the orbital frontal cortex. It turns out that these early relational experiences with caregivers (or lack thereof) are literally imprinted into infants' brain circuits.

In the case of the children in the foundling homes, they had very few interactions with an attachment figure, stunting the development of the brain circuits necessary for processing emotions and relational experiences. Many of these children got to the point where it was very difficult to process love—they didn't have the brain equipment necessary. Love fosters the brain conditions necessary to take in more love. What makes this even more significant is that these brain circuits go through a growth spurt in the first two to three years of life, so relational experiences in these first few years have far-reaching and long-lasting relational and spiritual effects. Negative effects, however, can be healed over time. This is all quite amazing when you stop and think about it. God made our brains such that we need healthy attachment relationships in order for them to grow and develop. God asks us to play a very real role in the development of others.

BECOMING ATTACHED TO GOD

On December 11, 2013, my wife, Liz, received a phone call from her physician just as she was about to take our kids to church. I was in the front yard saying goodbye. She walked around the car into the front yard and I could tell she was really trying to focus on the call. Whatever this was about, it was important. Then there was a moment I will never forget. As she was talking to the doctor, Liz hunched over as if she had been punched in the stomach, and a look came over her face that I had never seen before.

At that time we'd been married for twenty-one years, and I had seen a million looks on her face—but never this one. The best way I can describe the look is devastation mixed with fear and shock; it is the look you get when you've just been told you have cancer. We learned shortly after that it was stage 2 breast cancer.

When you experience a blow like this—especially a life threatening one—you quickly find out who your attachment figures are. These are the people you turn to for solace, comfort, and help in times of trouble. This was certainly one of the most severe times of trouble my wife and I had ever experienced. She went through two major surgeries, six months of chemotherapy, and three months of radiation treatments. An entire year of her life was taken up with treatment. Cancer became our lives.

The physical aspect was grueling. Liz could barely get up and walk for several days after the first surgery. She had tubes coming out of her that had to be drained every day. Chemotherapy was excruciatingly painful, difficult, and exhausting—Liz would feel sick for several days after the treatment. During many of those days, she couldn't even focus enough to read. All she could do was watch a movie, and when that proved too difficult she would try to sleep or simply stare into space. After several days, she would start to feel better and have a few decent days, only to go right back into another round of treatment and sickness.

On top of the physical pain and discomfort, the psychological aspect of having cancer and going through treatment was like being kicked when you're already down. Liz described it as living in an alternate universe. People treat you differently; often they don't know what to say and unintentionally say something insensitive. Then there's the loneliness. It's hard to explain to others what you're going through, so after a while you stop trying and feel more alone.

So how did Liz cope? Did she turn to God and relate to him as an attachment figure? Do we relate to God as an attachment figure—especially when we're distressed? Or do we move through life and difficulties not being vulnerable with God?

During her cancer treatment, Liz depended heavily on God and me for comfort and security. She developed a routine in which she would spend a significant amount of time with God in the morning. She read Scripture, prayed, and wrote in her journal. Most mornings she cried. In the evenings, we gathered as a family and spent time together eating dinner, playing games, and watching our favorite TV shows. As we watched our favorite shows, Liz always sat next to me and wanted to be in physical contact. She needed emotional and physical closeness. This was not a regression to an earlier developmental stage. Instead, it was a normal human need in the face of extreme distress. Thankfully, Liz was able to reach out and be vulnerable with God, me, and other important people in her life. This helped her cope, heal, and find meaning in her suffering.

Part of what it means to put your trust in Christ is to become attached to God. God is an attachment figure for us just like our human attachment figures. We seek to be close to God. We turn to God in times of trouble through prayer and often through lament. God becomes a haven of safety for us. As we become more secure in God's love and learn to rest in it, God becomes a secure base that empowers us to venture out into the world to do kingdom work. Understanding attachment, then, helps us understand how we experience and relate to God, especially with respect to comfort and emotional security.

There is significant evidence that most Christians do become attached to God and experience God as an attachment figure.[3] Just as with other attachment figures, we turn to God for comfort and safety when we're distressed. As the saying goes, "There are no atheists in foxholes." Attachment researchers note that God clearly fits the description of an attachment figure, and we can see this in numerous places throughout Scripture.

One biblical theme that speaks to our attachment to God is that of being adopted, through Christ, as children of God. In fact, the notion of adoption links an attachment-type relationship with God to our salvation. The New Testament uses legal images for salvation (e.g., justification[4]), and it also portrays salvation in very personal, relational terms such as *reconciliation* and *adoption*. Reconciliation suggests the idea that two people who were once enemies are brought into friendship. Through Christ, we become friends of God and this hints at the idea of attachment. However, the notion of adoption speaks even more clearly to our attachment to God. In Christ, we are adopted into God's family as sons and daughters. This is a major theme in the writings of both John and Paul. In Romans 8:15-16, for example, Paul writes, "So you have not received a spirit that makes you fearful slaves. Instead, you received God's Spirit when he adopted you as his own children. Now we call him, 'Abba, Father.' For his Spirit joins with our spirit to affirm that we are God's children."

All the images used in the New Testament for salvation reflect the same underlying reality—the believer's relationship with Christ through the Holy Spirit, and participation in the love among the Father, Son, and Spirit. And this relationship is described as a child-parent relationship. To be saved is by its very nature to be a child of God. A child-parent relationship is an attachment relationship *par excellence*, and so to be a child of God is to be attached to God. Understanding how attachment bonds work helps us flesh out the psychology of our relationship with God—how it should function and how it actually does function.

God doesn't just want us to come to him when we have our act together. He invites us to become attached, to turn to him in distress, to lament, to celebrate, and to call him "Abba" or "Daddy"—a term of affection for an attachment figure. This relationship with the triune God, through Christ, is the very essence of salvation, or eternal life. Salvation is a relationship with God in which he delights in being our *Abba*—with us in times of joy and in times of trouble, and being for us all the time.

HOW ATTACHMENT RELATIONSHIPS SHAPE OUR VIEW OF GOD

Jake, who we met at the beginning of this chapter, came to see me for therapy due to anxiety about his unstable relationship with his girlfriend.

When Jake was seven years old, his mom died in a tragic car accident. His father was supportive on a practical level, but emotionally distant. When Jake felt sad about his mother, his father would rationally explain that everyone dies at some point and this was simply his mother's "time." Jake's father showed very little empathy and wasn't able to connect to Jake's feelings of sadness and loss. His family rarely spoke of his mother after she died; his father just moved on with life as if nothing had happened, almost as if Jake's mom had never existed. Jake and his younger sister quickly learned that they were supposed to do the same. His father never stated it overtly, but Jake knew that it was not okay to feel sad and grieve the loss of his mother. If he wanted to maintain any connection to his only remaining attachment figure, he couldn't allow himself to feel sad.

This led to an attachment tendency or "filter" that was captured in a phrase Jake once told me: "Eventually, everyone will leave me." His attachment filter caused him to perceive women as not genuinely interested in him and to choose some women who ultimately weren't interested in him. In addition, he would become very anxious and need comfort from women who had little capacity to provide comfort. As part of an intricate attachment dance, which fulfilled Jake's expectations and worst fears, a number of romantic partners eventually *did* leave. This was, understandably, excruciatingly painful for Jake.

Jake also experienced a lot of anxiety in his relationship with God. He expected God to be emotionally distant, much like his father was. He would earnestly pray during a crisis, as if he had to be in a desperate situation to get God's attention. Even if he experienced some temporary relief, he would then withdraw from God and church to protect himself from the pain of impending abandonment. Jake's ingrained patterns of relating and feeling shaped all of his relationships, including his relationship with God.

Why did Jake's relationship with God seem to mirror his early family loss and ways of coping? And what does this mean for our relationship with God? Can we learn from Jake's story and somehow find a way to escape this influence? Maybe his story is an anomaly—or maybe we are destined to feel the pain of early relational wounds in our relationship with God.

If our relationship with God is an attachment relationship, then does it follow that we experience God similarly to the way we experience our primary human attachment figures? Or can we experience God as a loving attachment figure even when our human attachment figures fall short; does God fill in the gaps? The answer to both questions appears to be a qualified yes. The key to reconciling the two is to understand the *way* God fills in. Before we turn to this, however, it's important to point out that we all need God to "fill in the gaps" for us.

The answer to these questions is only a qualified yes because our human attachment bonds shape our God attachment bond, even in cases in which we experience insecure attachment or trauma. We might wonder, though: *Why don't we just know God is good?* Why doesn't this knowledge simply override our painful experiences with human attachment figures? The reason is that attachment to God is based on the relational knowledge we talked about in part two. It's a deep, implicit form of knowing that is crafted from our experiences with the human beings on whom we've depended for life, physical protection, and emotional security. Jake's attachment to God was shaped in profound ways by his early upbringing. But this is only part of the picture. Although our early attachment experiences with the people in our lives shape our attachment to God, they don't determine it. We can grow and change through new relational experiences with God and other important people in our lives.

There is a growing body of research that supports this idea that our relationship with God is significantly shaped by early attachment experiences and yet open to change.[5] The key to understanding how this works is to separate out the two ways of knowing—implicit knowledge (or internal spirituality) and explicit knowledge (or external spirituality). People's explicit knowledge of God/doctrine (and even spiritual practices) can be—and often is—inconsistent with their human attachment tendencies. However, people's implicit knowledge of God (experience of God and how they actually relate to God) typically corresponds well with their human attachment filters. This is something I've observed over and over again with my clients.

Julia, who we met in chapter four, exhibited both aspects of this (inconsistency at the explicit level, and consistency at the implicit level). When we interviewed Julia, she had graduated from college several years previously and was living in an urban area. She was involved in full-time ministry to her neighborhood. Julia referred to her family life growing up as "crazy." She stated:

> I grew up in a lot of poverty. Seeing some of the things I saw or a lot of the ways I was not provided for. A lot of neglect. All those kinds of things. My whole childhood was just a lot of trauma and so it's hard.

She continues, describing a vivid memory in which she realized the gravity of the pain in her family life:

> Things were really hard at home, and I can remember being a sixth grader or seventh grader and just thinking, things were just really sad . . . there wasn't a lot of joy there. I just remember this one moment of sitting at home and thinking, *This is crazy; this is the rest of my life.* It was just, I could tell there was something missing.

Despite Julia's insecure attachment history in her early family, she developed a robust external spirituality. She started attending youth group with a friend in the seventh grade, and the youth pastor and his wife mentored her. This helped Julia lay a foundation for her relationship with God. She became a leader in the youth group, attended church regularly, and studied the Bible and knew it well. On the outside, Julia was a model Christian for her age. From this perspective, we can see a disconnect between her early (insecure) attachment with her parents and her external spirituality. Her internal attachment filters were insecure and painful, and yet her external spirituality was strong. If you only looked at the surface level, you'd conclude that Julia was a spiritually mature believer for her age. But her explicit beliefs and external practices weren't integrated into her heart and the way she related and lived, and this became apparent over time.

As I mentioned earlier, Julia hit an empty, dark period in which she gradually became aware of a disconnect between her external faith that appeared "together" and her internal faith that was entering a free fall of emptiness and disillusionment. In the latter years of high school, in the midst of this emptiness, she tried to be the Christian she once was. "But I kept failing," she said. This continued into college and came to a head her sophomore year, at camp, where she cried out to God. Just as Julia felt her parents had left her, she also felt God had left her.

Reflecting on why she went through this dark time, Julia implicitly made this connection: "I think there was a lot of deep hurt." Her painful experiences with her parents became an insecure attachment filter that also applied to God. When we look beneath the surface, we see that her true experience of God, her attachment to God, reflected her painful, insecure attachment filters with her parents.

A growing body of research is corroborating this idea that our attachment to God generally parallels our human attachment filters at the implicit or experiential level.[6] The overall research findings suggest that when we look at the relational dynamics of our spirituality—our implicit relational knowledge—our patterns with God parallel those with our human attachment figures. However, our attachment dynamics don't generally predict dimensions of our spirituality that have more to do with our explicit knowledge. We have more intentional control over this and over our commitments. This is good, because, as we will see, it allows us to actively participate in facilitating the conditions we need to grow. It's important to understand, however, that explicit knowledge doesn't directly or immediately change our gut-level dynamics with God.

Some people, when they hear this idea, fear this means that their relationship with God can never grow beyond the maturity of their early human relationships. But both research and experience suggest that our relationship with God can change or grow beyond whatever relational shortcomings we inevitably experienced in childhood. Transformation in our relationship with God comes about directly through our relational experiences with God and others. We are loved into loving.

Furthermore, because our soul, or heart, is unified, it means that this kind of change happens at the core of our soul and flows out into all our relationships. Changes in our relationship with God tend to coincide with changes in our human relationships, and vice versa, because they reflect deep changes at the very center of our soul.

Although we all struggle with some painful experiences that negatively affect our attachment to God, there is hope for change and growth. We'll return to this in more detail in part four on transformation, but first I want to go back to Jake's story. Here we see that attachment is not only fundamental to what it means to be human, but it also has the power to transform us.

TRANSFORMATION THROUGH ATTACHMENT

Over time Jake and I developed an attachment bond. It didn't happen overnight, but gradually I saw the three aspects of attachment showing up in our relationship. As Jake became more vulnerable with me over time, he experienced me as a *haven of safety* when he was distressed. When he became extremely anxious, Jake would call me and ask to have an extra session that week. This was a very vulnerable and scary thing to do. How would I respond? Would I dismiss his needs or take them seriously? Even more than in a normal session, he was reaching out and saying, "I need you." As he experienced me being responsive and empathic in these cases, his anxiety diminished and he felt better. I became a haven of safety for him.

Jake wanted to be *close*, both in terms of consistent therapy times and in the sense of emotional contact. When there was a rift between us, or when I would miss a session because I was sick or traveling, Jake would become distressed and would miss me. In the beginning of therapy, he didn't feel this way; he looked at me more as a professional who could dispense wise advice to him. But then it became clear that this had changed. I was gone at a conference for a week, and when we met after this Jake told me—for the first time—that he missed me. Something inside him had shifted. I was no longer just his "Tuesday at 6:00." He wanted to be close because he became attached to me, and I to him. This was a manifestation of an invisible bond.

Through the many times of experiencing comfort, Jake gradually developed an internal sense of security, a *secure base*. He started to feel secure within himself because he internalized my care. He knew at a deep emotional level that I was there for him and he began to carry this inside him. This, in turn, began to transform his experience of God. He began to feel that it was possible to feel connected to God, so in faith he began to take steps to reach out more to God. In doing so, Jake started to feel that God was there—that God knew him and maybe had actually been there all along. In the later stages of therapy, Jake gave me a cross with a heart cut out of it. He kept the heart and told me it represented the care from me that he now carries inside. In many ways, Jake is a changed person (and so am I) because of an invisible bond that reflects the very heart and love of the Trinity.

We all need attachment relationships to grow, heal, and find meaning in our lives. These early relational bonds have a profound impact on our souls. We innately seek to create invisible attachment bonds with caregivers by seeking proximity and emotional closeness, comfort when distressed, and a secure base from which to venture out and explore the world. Our attachment experiences, both positive and painful, become encoded in our brain circuits, which then filter our experiences with important people and God.

Thankfully, the story of our development doesn't end in childhood. We continue to need attachment relationships with others throughout life, and new, loving attachment-type experiences can transform how we view ourselves, others, and God.

But what do these attachment relationships look like? It turns out that there are three broad patterns of attachment, to which we now turn.

8

How We Connect *to* God *and* Others

JAKE'S ATTACHMENT FILTER was revealed by his statement, "Eventually, everyone will leave me." This is a version of what attachment researchers call a *preoccupied* (or *anxious*) attachment pattern. But it's not the only attachment pattern. Although each of our relational dynamics with God and others is unique, we gain important insights by clustering these patterns into larger categories. Some people, like Jake, cope with painful childhood experiences by kicking their attachment system into overdrive. They become anxious and cling to others, always on the lookout for expected rejection.

Others cope by shutting down their attachment system and running away when others get too close. Doug was very isolated and had no meaningful sense of connection to God. He had also recently ended a brief romantic relationship. None of this particularly bothered him, which was part of the problem. In addition, he was also not doing well in the practical ministry aspects of his seminary training. After a psychological assessment required by his program revealed a high degree of isolation, difficulty maintaining close relationships, irritability, and a sense of emptiness (the latter two symptoms are associated with atypical depression among men[1]), his adviser strongly encouraged him to seek out therapy.

At this request, Doug came to see me for therapy, but he wasn't sure why he needed it. He made it clear to me in the first session that he knew quite a bit about psychology (perhaps more than I did!) and that he was quite capable of managing his life on his own.

Doug had grown up in an emotional desert. His father was a high-level executive who was overly rational and had strong narcissistic traits. His mother was devaluing in a passive-aggressive way. To protect himself from the pain of unmet needs and the anger of being devalued, Doug developed a concept of himself as being superior to others. This is a variant of what attachment researchers call a *dismissing* attachment pattern.

Over the first months of therapy it became quite clear to me that Doug had a very detached relationship with God. He was smart and committed to his faith, but he couldn't tolerate true intimacy even with God. God was an idea "out there," not a person with whom to develop a close, trusting relationship. Whereas with Jake I felt needed, with Doug I felt devalued. I suspected most of the people in his life felt devalued by him.

In contrast to Jake and Doug, others grow up in a safe relational environment and don't need to either hyperactivate or shut down their attachment needs. They develop a *secure* attachment early in life. Andrew, who we'll meet in a moment, grew up with secure, loving parents. He learned at an early age that he could trust his parents to be emotionally available and to comfort him when he was distressed. As a result, he felt comfortable with his attachment needs and developed the ability to form close relationships with others and God.

Both Jake and Doug experienced emotional pain in their childhoods, but they coped in very different ways. As a result, they had very different dynamics in their relationship with God. Their patterns were also quite different from Andrew's relational dynamics with God.

Why do we see these very different patterns of relationship with others and God? Some people become anxious and others distant; some seem to have a natural ability to trust people and form close relationships. Are there other patterns? How can we learn from these and grow to develop healthy, secure attachments?

Patterns develop as people cope with their particular relational environments. Looking closely we find multiple variations, but research and clinical experience suggest there are at least three main strategies of attachment patterns, with several subtypes. I often refer to these patterns as "filters" because they filter our experiences in relationships— biasing our perceptions, filtering out the unfamiliar, and selecting the familiar. These patterns shape our capacity to love God and others in profound ways, but they are always open to change. They reflect the basic way we connect as human beings. Though they will always be flawed this side of heaven, attachment bonds reflect the essence of what it means to be human. Let's take a look at the three main attachment filters along with some key subtypes within them.

Secure Attachment Filter

Some people develop a secure attachment to God early on due to healthy attachment bonds with their caregivers. Andrew, an undergraduate student I interviewed for a research project, is an example.

When I met Andrew at my office to interview him, he was a junior majoring in biology. He had grown up in a Christian home in Oregon. His parents were still married and he described them as supportive and loving.

I asked Andrew if he experienced anxiety in his relationship with God, or fear that God won't be there for him. He responded:

I feel like there have not been many times with my relationship with God where I feel like, okay, he is not going to be there for me. I don't know if that comes just from so much, from . . . if the naturalness of that comes from my parents. My parents have just been so supportive of everything and like from the small things to like sports games and stuff to like me even being out here at [college] and they are just so, so supportive and so, yeah caring, so then it's just easy to look at the Lord and of course the Lord is going to be there because there has not been any major relationship where someone didn't come through that I was really impacted by and that I really needed to depend on them.

Andrew clearly had a secure attachment to his parents and to God. This security seems to have developed at a young age with his parents, and now he experiences that same security with God.

This provides a secure base for Andrew to be aware of his sin and struggles, to experience God's forgiveness, and in turn, to forgive and love others. For example, when I asked Andrew about the area of forgiveness in his life, he told me he had been talking a lot with a mentor about the difference between knowing you're forgiven versus feeling forgiven. Here's how he described it:

> I think what the process usually looks like is . . . a process of repentance, and even after repenting there is not usually a sense of repentance. It usually comes almost as time goes on and I get into the Word more, or even just thinking about a worship song, or a hymn, or thinking about something that contains truth. . . . That feeling of forgiveness usually comes after that or, often after telling myself and going over . . . 1 John 1:9, "confess our sins for he is faithful and just to forgive us our sins." It is usually meditating on that truth that then brings a feeling of forgiveness. And I think how that works with forgiving other people . . . I feel like I have sinned a lot and I feel like I know the Lord has forgiven me so much that looking at that makes it easy to forgive other people.

Andrew has a healthy awareness of his own sin and actively engages in a process of repenting and reflecting on God's forgiveness. His underlying security in God and others is part of what enables him to be aware of his own shortcomings and sin. This whole process helps him to experience God's forgiveness and not just know it in his head. This, in turn, helps him forgive others. Andrew has his struggles, but his security in God developed as a young child because of his secure attachment to his parents, and this led to a gradual, stable process of spiritual growth.

Other people, like Julia, have to develop a secure attachment to God over time as they heal from the pain of insecure attachment bonds from their caregivers. As Julia's faith bottomed out, something new started to grow. She had a mentor that summer who helped her start to work through her spiritual breakdown. She said:

> I remember it first started off with me just starting to be real honest with the Lord about how I felt and not trying to pretend like everything was okay. So that's kind of how it started and then [my mentor] made me promise that when I came back to college that I'd find mentors that can walk through the process with me.

Julia did find mentors, and this led to a reconstructive process of "learning to be a believer all over again" as she put it. She continued:

> Now I have a relationship with [God] where I realize all these things that I do aren't just something to check off my list or make him happy or to please him or to be this great person on the outside for everyone else to admire but instead like all these things are disciplines . . . they are avenues for me to get to know him more. Everything has just been completely turned upside down in regards to how I see my faith and how I see that being lived out.

Julia's youth pastor and his wife, and other mentors, helped God's love to stick. It doesn't stick perfectly by any stretch, but it sticks. Today, Julia has a secure attachment to God and she is thriving spiritually, despite a traumatic background and insecure attachment in her childhood.

The breadth of research on secure attachment reveals a strikingly coherent picture of an organized strategy for approaching relationships and emotional meaning.[2] A secure attachment filter develops when we have repeated experiences with caregivers who are consistently emotionally available and responsive. And as noted above, this can come at any point in life and from anyone who becomes an attachment figure. This is the "haven of safety." From these experiences, we learn a strategy for regulating emotions that allows us to be aware of our emotions and to gain support from others in a balanced way. Like Andrew and Julia, we learn that our own emotions won't overwhelm us, and that expressing emotions to others will lead to a positive connection.

Secure attachment bonds help us to learn that we are capable of managing distress with the help of others and that others will provide comfort when we need it. For example, research shows that when secure women feel anxious, they are more likely to seek support than less secure women.[3] In addition, secure women tend to feel comforted by support from their romantic partners, whereas less secure women tend to withdraw emotionally and physically from their partners when they are distressed.

Because you know others will be there for you if you become distressed, you develop an internal "secure base." This is what Andrew had with his parents and Julia developed with her youth pastors. This provides the confidence to explore your external and internal world. These experiences are recorded in implicit memory and then used to filter your relational experiences, particularly those with whom you have some measure of close connection or attachment, including God.

As we saw with Andrew and Julia, people with secure attachment filters bring these patterns into their relationship with God.[4] This doesn't mean there won't be difficult and painful times in their relationship with God. Rather, it means that they tend to expect God to be available and responsive, to genuinely care about them, and to welcome the expression of emotion, including negative emotions.

In our study mentioned previously, we found strong support for this. Secure individuals showed a stronger sense of connection to a spiritual community than any of the insecure attachment groups.[5] In addition, they experienced less anxiety in their relationship with God than people with preoccupied and dismissing tendencies. This allows secure individuals to process difficult experiences in relationship with God, and to stay connected to God even in the midst of dark and difficult times. Such times may be due to life situations or they may be times when God seems unresponsive—what St. John of the Cross described as the "dark night of the soul" when one feels God is absent.[6] Regardless of the nature of the difficult experience, a secure attachment filter provides a secure base to process and grow through trials.

In an interview-based study, Australian researcher Marie-Therese Proctor identified six indicators of secure attachment to God. What's particularly interesting, though, is that she found three of these indicators showed up much more frequently than the other three: positive God concept, positive relationship with God, and valuing of relationship with God. Significantly less interview material was coded for the other indicators—recognizing doubting as a part of a healthy relationship, comfort with questioning and examining beliefs, and integration (the ability to reflectively embrace and integrate positive and negative life experiences within one's spiritual framework and relationship with God).[7] Proctor noted the intriguing possibility of a developmental progression in one's secure attachment to God. It seems likely there is a substantial range of developmental maturity within each attachment category with respect to relationship with God, and Proctor's results may be picking up on this.

For example, it may be that some people can have a foundational level of security, but don't have the capacity to process doubts and trials in more healthy ways. The ability to regulate our emotions and view things from multiple perspectives may be necessary to process doubt and painful experiences in more complex and mature ways. The developmental path starts by building a basic sense of security and trust in God. Then as we mature in faith, this security deepens and becomes more complex and robust, allowing us to face questions and doubts head on. This happens largely through facing trials in the context of loving relationships within a community—as we'll read in part four when we learn about transformation.

PREOCCUPIED ATTACHMENT FILTER

As we saw earlier, Jake had a preoccupied or anxious attachment filter. Ever since his mother died (and left him, in a sense) he felt that others would eventually leave as well. The loss was difficult enough, but made even more difficult because Jake's father wasn't consistently responsive to his needs for comfort. He would sometimes respond initially when Jake was upset, but at a certain point he would shut down and withdrawal emotionally, leaving Jake to cope by himself. Some people, like Jake, develop a *helpless* type of preoccupied attachment, characterized by relating to others in a deferential, helpless manner in order to evoke comfort on a superficial level. Others develop an *angry, chaotic* type of preoccupied attachment. Often stemming from unresolved trauma, these people tend to feel chaotic and empty inside, which leads them to experience life as an ongoing crisis. There are other subtypes and variations in how this looks, but the various types of preoccupied anxious attachment have common features.[8]

Jake, like others with an anxious attachment filter, expected others to be unreliable.[9] In his mind, sometimes others may be available and responsive, and sometimes they may not be. He never knew how this would play out, which produced a lot of anxiety. People with this attachment tendency develop a strategy of hyperactivating—shifting into high gear—their need for others when they become distressed. The strategy here is to try to pull attachment figures into providing comfort and care. There is a tendency for people with this filter to become preoccupied with unresolved emotional pain, and to demand—either implicitly or explicitly—that others help them manage their pain. This self-preoccupation also makes it understandably difficult to notice and attend to others' needs, which is necessary to effectively love others, linking attachment back to our core concern of spiritual transformation.

Jake had easy access to painful emotions; however, he had difficulty managing his emotions, which is common for those with preoccupied attachment tendencies. For example, preoccupied individuals recall negative memories more quickly and strongly than people with any other attachment filter.[10] They also experience all emotions as very intense, regardless of whether they are the primary emotion associated with a particular memory. If Jake recalls a sad memory, this tends to cause emotional flooding, bringing up his anxiety as well. These folks often become overwhelmed with their negative emotions.

The way preoccupied individuals disclose information about themselves also fits their organized strategy for dealing with attachment relationships and emotions. They disclose about the same amount of personal information as securely attached individuals. But they have difficulty adapting the level of their self-disclosure to situational cues. Jake, for example, would sometimes share too much information early on in a relationship.

In addition, unlike secure individuals, they generally don't respond in kind to others by disclosing things on the same topic.[11] What's revealing, though, is that they tend to like high disclosure conversations. This is a complex pattern of self-disclosure that represents an organized (although not conscious) strategy for dealing with close attachment relationships, emotion, and distress. Jake, like others with this attachment filter, tended to: (1) focus on his own needs and feelings in an understandable effort to regulate them; (2) disclose too much information to people with whom he wasn't very close; and (3) respond to others in a way that didn't match how much the other person had shared. Sadly, this pattern sometimes led Jake to become attached to romantic partners who weren't healthy.

People with a secure attachment filter tend to seek out new information and adjust their beliefs and expectations to account for that information. Jake, like those with a preoccupied attachment filter, didn't do this. Early on in therapy, he had difficulty taking in new positive relational experiences, hindering his ability to revise his implicit beliefs based on new information. This is common among people with preoccupied attachment tendencies.[12] For example, in their evaluations of themselves, they tend to focus on their weaknesses. This creates a lot of internal distress, which in turn exacerbates their negative view of themselves.[13] In addition, preoccupied individuals are less likely than secure individuals to revise their perception of their partner, even when their partner behaves in ways that don't fit their gut-level expectations.[14] This contributes to a cycle of negative relational patterns.

What does all this mean for Jake's relationship with God? His preoccupied attachment tendencies operated in his relationship with God, just as they do for others with this attachment pattern. These individuals are prone to feel abandoned by God and to experience their relationship with God as unstable. This was a painful recurring theme in therapy with Jake. He often felt abandoned by God, and this led to instability in his spiritual practices. He would start attending church and engaging in basic spiritual disciplines, and then withdrawal from God when an event brought anxiety back to the surface.

In the study my colleagues and I conducted, we found that individuals with preoccupied attachment tendencies had less of a sense of connection to their spiritual community and more anxiety in their relationship with God than secure individuals.[15] Other research indicates that preoccupied individuals view God as less loving than those with positive views of themselves.[16] They tend to engage in clingy, help-seeking forms of prayer, desperately seeking to hold on to a bond that feels very fragile.[17] The pain they experience in their relationship with God becomes part of the overall emotional pain in their lives. If something touches on a painful nerve in one area of their life, it will often spill over into some aspect of their relationship with God, and vice versa.

Those with preoccupied attachment tendencies need God and their spiritual community to help them manage their emotions. This is normal and healthy up to a certain point, but it can get out of balance when these individuals don't feel like the help offered is sufficient. In order to grow, they need help regulating their emotions. This is something that can be provided in a healthy spiritual community, but it requires sacrifice, commitment, and genuine love on the part of those in the community. At times, professional therapy is needed in addition to a supportive spiritual community. In Proctor's study of attachment to God, she found that profiles of preoccupied individuals showed indications of self-doubt and concerns about their value to God.[18] In short, individuals with a preoccupied attachment filter tend to experience a significant degree of anxiety in their relationship with God. In our church communities, we need to foster a greater awareness of how we can help our brothers and sisters in Christ who struggle with anxious attachment tendencies.

Dismissing Attachment Filter

Doug, who we met earlier, exhibited a *devaluing* type of dismissing attachment. He learned to protect himself from the pain of his unmet needs by thinking more highly of himself than others. One illustration of this is that he conveyed to me the sense that he knew more about psychology and therapy than I did. This superior attitude is not particularly endearing to the person on the other end of the relationship—it certainly wasn't to me. I had to work hard to get past this attitude and find a way to connect with Doug.

The illusion of specialness Doug created eventually dissolved, proving to be a hollow substitute for meaningful human connection. Yet genuine intimacy risked exposing deep feelings of longing that his parents wouldn't tolerate. So Doug understandably felt trapped. His response to me, and to all potentially close relationships, was like that of a "starving man at a banquet who tells himself the food just isn't good enough and therefore refuses to eat."[19] He would often dismiss my attempts to be empathic and then explain a psychological theory to me. "I don't think you really understand," he would tell me.

It's a bit maddening to be in relationship with someone who devalues you. But it's important to remember that this protected Doug from a very deep sense of shame—the feeling that he was never good enough for his parents, that he was fundamentally defective in some way that he could never quite get right. Like all unhealthy attachment patterns, this one protected Doug, but at a cost. It was self-defeating because it sabotaged his relationships. Doug pushed me away because if I mattered to him, I could hurt him, and most of the important people in his life had hurt him. So his gut told him that I would surely do the same.

While Doug displayed a devaluing type of dismissing attachment, others develop an *idealizing* pattern. Those with idealizing tendencies find they can obtain some sense of connection, however fragile, by satisfying their parents' needs. Often growing up with self-absorbed, insecure parents, they make an unspoken deal with their parents: in exchange for admiration and making their parents feel special, they receive a derivative sense of specialness, which turns out to be quite hollow. It's hollow because it isn't safe to truly be emotionally dependent on their parents or to be their authentic selves. These individuals develop a mutual admiration society with those close to them, allowing them to avoid true, healthy dependency.

Still others develop a more *controlling* form of dismissing attachment. These folks turn most relationships into a power struggle. They often grow up with controlling parents who are uncomfortable with close physical affection. They resist their parents' control by fighting against the feeling of powerlessness—a move that also protects them from the perceived dangerous pursuit of connection and comfort. The loss of control can threaten the person's identity, self-sufficiency, or autonomy. The underlying strategy for all three of these variations of dismissing attachment is the same—to detach from one's feelings and shut down the need for others in order to protect against emotional dependency and intimacy. Research is shedding light on some of the general characteristics of those with dismissing attachment tendencies.

Since they don't develop a sense of felt security from their caregivers, people like Doug find another way to comfort themselves—one that doesn't require emotionally connected relationships. By deactivating their need for others, their brains become wired to regulate their emotions by themselves.[20] In other words, people with dismissing attachment tendencies distance themselves from sources of distress and potentially frustrating attachment figures, and cut off negative emotions and thoughts. Also, like Doug, they develop a conscious image of themselves as strong, highly self-reliant, and above needing other people. They tend to view people who need others as weak, which is part of why Doug was so resistant to therapy. From one perspective we can see this as a creative adaptation to feeling emotionally alone. However, this strategy backfires in terms of their ability to process emotions, and develop and maintain healthy relationships. This unconscious strategy comes at a high cost.

Unlike securely attached individuals who can access and tolerate their painful emotions with relative ease, and preoccupied individuals who experience a flood of painful emotions when one comes online, people with dismissing tendencies keep themselves at arm's length from their emotional world by keeping all emotions at bay.[21] They have less accessibility to memories of sadness or anxiety than either secure or preoccupied individuals. They also tend to deny experiencing anger and yet show more intense physiological signs of anger and hostility. There is a major disconnect here, and this is precisely the cost of their attachment strategy. If you ask them about anger, they'll tell you that other people around them are angry, but they're not.[22]

Just as Doug avoided close relationships, he also didn't disclose much personal information to others, a common trait among those with dismissing tendencies.[23] As we would expect, dismissing individuals are less satisfied with their relationships than secure individuals, and this may be due to the fact that revealing important things about yourself is necessary for intimacy.[24] We also know that dismissing individuals avoid conflict more than people with a secure attachment filter, and show more stonewalling behavior (cutting off communication) in romantic relationships.[25]

Doug's attachment patterns played out in his relationship with God.[26] He would consciously acknowledge needing God, but he rarely actually relied on God in difficult times. When they are distressed, people with dismissing attachment tendencies generally continue self-reliant coping strategies, keeping God and their spiritual community on the periphery, while relying on themselves and their explicit knowledge about God. For example, we found that dismissing individuals experienced less of a sense of belonging to a spiritual community than secure individuals.[27] They also have fewer spiritual friendships—those that intentionally foster spiritual growth—than secure individuals.

Another interesting finding is that dismissing individuals sometimes respond to a disruption in an important relationship by increasing religious behaviors or involvement.[28] This contradicts their normal strategy. It seems likely that they may initially react to such distress with their typical strategy of deactivating their felt need for closeness. However, if the stress gets too severe, and too disorganizing, this may render their normal way of coping (short circuiting painful emotions) ineffective, leading to a flood of painful emotions. This in turn may drive them to God and their spiritual community for support and comfort. We know that the hyperactivation and deactivation strategies both serve the same function of regulating our emotions, so it may be that each strategy serves as a backup for the other when it becomes overwhelmed by high levels of stress that push a person out of their normal pathways of coping.

Dismissing people tend to engage in types of prayer that minimize a sense of closeness to God.[29] In fact, when they become more distressed and need more support (even though they don't show it), dismissing individuals spend even less time in types of prayer that foster emotional connection with God. When Doug and I talked about his spiritual life, this became evident. When he was most distressed, Doug became more emotionally distant from God. It was understandably difficult for him to be vulnerable. Like others with this attachment pattern, Doug kept God at arm's length emotionally, and related to God mainly through explicit knowledge. Even though they can change, these attachment filters are pervasive. Let's take a look at why they're so stubborn.

WHY ATTACHMENT FILTERS ARE STUBBORN

First, our attachment filters are the only way we know how to create a connection with others. Originally, these attachment filters were necessary to cope with and maximize a sense of relational connection with our attachment figures. Jake's helped him cope with parents who abandoned him in different ways—his mother through death and his father by not helping him grieve. Our filters help us adapt to the realities of our relational environment, then they become *entrenched pathways* in our brains and ways of relating. When the attachment is insecure, we learn to adapt to less-than-ideal relationships.

To illustrate how this happens in our brains, imagine approaching a field with high grass. You need to cross the field, so you pick a spot and walk through and trample down the grass. When the next person approaches the field and sees the path trampled down, they'll most likely walk through the path that you created, because it's the path of least resistance. When they walk through, they further trample the grass. With each successive person, it becomes more likely that they will cross through the same pathway. Our brains work in a similar way when it comes to memory. Repeated experiences with attachment figures become ingrained in implicit memory through changes in the biochemical structures in the brain. This makes it more likely that the filter will be activated in the future.

As a result, we bring old adaptations to new situations and relational experiences with God and others, because this is the only way we know how, at a gut level, to connect with others. And because we are prewired to connect, any kind of connection that's familiar, even if distorted and painful, gets tagged in our brains as better than no connection at all. Leaving our attachment filters behind can feel overwhelming and scary, and it's not an option under our conscious control because of the way our brains process implicit relational knowledge. Psychoanalyst Stephen Mitchell suggested that people cannot give up old, dysfunctional attachments until new, healthier attachments are emerging to take their place.[30]

This is the process I see taking place in my therapy work with clients. Attachment filters aren't something we just opt out of because we're no longer satisfied. Relationships, and the residues of them that we carry within, are quite simply part of the very fabric of our souls and what it means to be human.

Mary Main, a leading attachment theorist proposed the idea of "secondary felt security," which sheds some light on the stubborn nature of attachment filters.[31] Even though insecure attachment filters are painful, they provide a sense of felt security in a secondary way. We're primarily motivated by human contact and connection—even if it's painful contact. The painful connection of an insecure attachment filter provides some form of security because it's the emotionally familiar territory of connection. Secondary felt security is better than no security at all.

Second, our attachment filters are stubborn because they operate in a way that is *self-reinforcing*. We're prone to filter our experiences through the pathways of our attachment patterns because those are engrained in our brains. When this happens, it affects what we *perceive* from others in our relationships so that we end up playing a role in reinforcing our own filters, as was the case with Jake. For example, depressed people have a decreased ability to detect facial emotion— brain imaging studies show that depressed people have less blood flow in the right hemisphere where facially expressed emotion is processed.[32] Even if someone is supportive, depression will cause people to have difficulty picking this up at an implicit level, so they have difficulty using the facial expressions of others to help them feel better and change their filters. This further intensifies the person's depressed state and attachment filter.

Our filters not only affect our relational perceptions—how we interpret experiences at an automatic gut level—they also influence how other people relate to us. We respond to others based on the way our experiences are run through our attachment filters. For example, the depressed person who can't pick up contingent, supportive emotions on a friend's face then starts to feel more worthless and unlovable. This in turn may cause the person to either lash out in anger or withdraw. As you can imagine, when the friend tries to reach out in support, but gets either an outburst of anger or withdrawal in response, it doesn't foster further relational connection. In fact, it creates just the opposite. Now the friend is likely to respond to the depressed person in anger or by pulling away. And this creates a negative cycle that reinforces the depressed person's attachment filters. He feels that, once again, people are not there for him.

When it comes to the negative aspects of our attachment filters, we work against our own growth and healing because we're trying to connect in the only way we know how. This isn't a conscious choice we're making in the moment; there are just no other ways of connecting on our radar. These relational cycles play out over and over in our lives and are difficult to change. We're dependent on God and others to show us a different way of connecting that's healthier and more loving.

In this chapter, we saw that attachment patterns become engrained in our souls and shape the way we connect to others. There are several broad patterns of attachment that shape our relationships: secure attachment (in which people feel comfortable with closeness and seek out support) and insecure attachment in two major variants—preoccupied (hyperactivation of attachment needs) and dismissing (deactivation of attachment needs). Insecure attachment patterns often create a negative cycle that is difficult to change.

Thankfully, this is not the end of the story. Our attachment tendencies can be transformed into an "intimate and continuous relationship" with attachment figures.[33] In a time when nearly half of Americans are reporting loneliness and disconnection is becoming an epidemic, this is what we all need.[34] We need healthy attachment bonds that give us a place to find comfort, the confidence to explore, and the love of the Trinity to share with the world. The next step in our journey is to explore the goal and process of transformation.

PART FOUR

TRANSFORMATION

Born *to* Love

"I can't believe my dad!"

This common refrain kicked off a session with my client Daniel, who often became very frustrated with his father's attempts to love him. Earlier in the week, Daniel's dad showed up at his door unannounced with "more stuff" he had purchased for Daniel and his children. Daniel was surprised and frustrated because they didn't need any of this stuff. While they appreciated the thought behind it, his children didn't even like the clothes their grandfather had purchased for them. What's worse, due to some chronic health issues, Daniel easily became over-stimulated. He needed the house to be uncluttered—all these things were simply more clutter. He had tried to explain this to his father on multiple occasions, but to no avail.

This last incident was the straw that broke the camel's back. Despite being very nervous about it, Daniel talked to his dad about this pattern. He explained that while he was grateful for the efforts, he didn't need these things and the clutter was causing stress. He also told his dad that he felt like he didn't really listen or know him well. His dad's response was: "I was only trying to help; I'm not sure why you're being so sensitive about this." After this guilt trip, Daniel understandably came into session fuming mad.

Daniel's dad was genuinely trying to love his son, and thought he was, but he was unaware of his own attachment tendencies and the impact of his actions. Sometimes our love falls short, despite our best intentions. How is it that we can think we're loving someone when in reality we're not actually helping and may even be hurting the other person? If love doesn't only depend on our intentions, then how do we know if we're truly loving another person? And how do we grow in our love for God and others?

First, we have to have a clear understanding of what love is, beyond our culture's thin view of romantic love. We need to understand the nature of love in order to grow in our ability to love, which is the ultimate goal of spiritual transformation. Second, we need to discern how to love others well in the particulars of any given relationship and situation, while taking into account our own attachment tendencies. We'll start with the nature of love, and then turn to the art of love.

THE NATURE OF LOVE

There are two essential components of love that can guide us through our murky motivations so that our attempts to love actually *are* loving. The first is desiring and pursuing the good of the other, and the second is desiring and pursuing union or connection with the other.[1]

Among the diverse usages of the word *love*, one of the most prominent meanings is that of seeking the good of the other. For example, Stephen Post's definition of love centers on affirming and delighting in the *well-being* of others.[2] This is not a sense of happiness or well-being that focuses on pleasure, but rather something closer to what the Greeks called *eudaimonia,* which refers to flourishing or virtuousness. The well-being that love seeks to promote is similar to what the Sermon on the Mount refers to as *makarios*. While this word is most often translated as "blessed," *makarios* likely refers more to human flourishing—a Christian parallel to Aristotle's concept of *eudaimonia.*[3] For simplicity, we might call this "health of the soul." Whatever term we use, love is essentially about desiring and working toward what is objectively good for the other, according to God's design of human nature.

Working toward the good of another requires enough knowledge of that person to know what would be good for them. We also need to bear in mind what kind of relationship we have with them. Love as a desire for the well-being of others is common in all kinds of relationships— friendships, romantic relationships, parent-child relationships, love of neighbor, and even love of enemy. As we'll see, the good we bestow must be appropriate to that particular relationship. Working toward the good of another also requires a secure attachment filter; when our filters are insecure, our actions toward others are often motivated more by our own needs, even if we desire to act in loving ways.

If the good we desire and carry out toward loved ones doesn't promote well-being for the other, then our love is most likely falling short in some way, as was the case with Daniel's dad. When this happens, we may not have sufficient knowledge of the other, or we may not be attending to the kind of relationship we have with that person.

Sometimes this ill-conceived love takes the form of well-meaning gifts like with Daniel's father. In other cases, it involves well-meaning help or protection that actually ends up harming the person. A college student client came to see me because he was struggling with depression. It turns out his parents were regulating and controlling every aspect of his life in their effort to protect him from the negative forces of society. A very strict curfew and extremely limited social outlets led to increasing depression and growing resentment against his parents. Their intentions were good, but they failed to appreciate his social and emotional needs.

In *The Four Loves*, C. S. Lewis recounts a similar example of Mrs. Fidget.[4] She stays up late for her children, makes dinner for them, and generally attempts to meet their every need, even as they become adults. Her "generosity" isn't offered freely; rather, it is forced on them, an implicit condition for relationship. Her insistence on complete dependence is ultimately serving her own interests and not the good of her children. As Alexander Pruss puts it, her love isn't "humble." It doesn't defer to the actual needs of her children and, therefore, it isn't truly loving.

While we can be mistaken about what promotes the good of the other, sometimes the other can be mistaken about what will be good for themselves. Loving doesn't always entail giving people what they want. Rather, it involves desiring and doing what we can to accomplish what is truly in the best interest of the loved one; what really contributes to his or her flourishing. And, of course, sometimes we're mistaken about what we need to flourish. We can see this clearly in the contexts of parenting and psychotherapy.

Children may want certain freedoms or possessions that will harm them, despite what they think. As our kids got older they realized that both their parents are psychologists and that this has implications for their lives. When our older son, Brennan, was about 9 years old, he was riding in the back of the car with his good friend Josh, also the son of a psychologist. They were lamenting about their parents being psychologists when Brennan said: "Yeah, it sucks because they know all the research, so they don't let you do anything fun." There was a time, for instance, when many of their friends and classmates were playing violent video games and they really wanted to play them as well. We didn't allow it because we believed that it wasn't good for their well-being.

Clients understandably want to avoid processing emotionally painful issues, which is not in their best interest in the long run. Mary came to see me due to conflict with her husband. Beneath this, however, was unresolved anger and grief about her mother's depression and neglect of her when she was young. At some point in the therapy I realized that we hadn't talked much about how her mother's depression affected her. When I tried to make connections between this and some of her other relational difficulties, she didn't have much to say. She would stay on the surface and change the subject. At some level Mary didn't want to talk about her mother's depression because she was scared of what she'd find there. I could have avoided the subject altogether, but that was not in Mary's best interest. So I continued to bring up the subject and gently help her process the pain of growing up with a profoundly depressed mother. In love, we provide what others truly need for their good, not necessarily what they want. This is often difficult and requires a lot of discernment and sometimes sacrifice.

Seeking the well-being of the other may take a number of forms, depending on the needs of the other. Where there are needs or suffering, love will move us to respond with compassion, sometimes in sacrificial ways, to meet those needs. Where there is injustice, love moves to promote justice, to provide and protect basic human rights. Love seeks the well-being of the loved one in all its interrelated dimensions: spiritual, emotional, social, vocational, physical, and financial.

Philosopher Eleonore Stump argues that the ultimate good, the thing that ultimately leads to flourishing, is loving connection with God and sharing this loving connection with others.[5] The fact that the ultimate good for us is loving relational connection illustrates the centrality of relational capacities for love, and ties back to attachment. Love is never a detached act, a rational calculation of what will promote the good of the other. In its purest form, love requires deep connection and secure attachment, or the desire for such a connection, which is a form of relational knowledge. There is an intrinsic link between goodwill and connection; they go together by their very nature. Connection is the most profound "good" we can seek for another, especially a shared connection with God.

This leads us to the second component of love: desiring and pursuing connection, or union, with the other. One aspect of loving connection is sharing in the life-affirming goals of the other, which requires understanding the other's perspective to some extent.

For the past few years, my son Brennan has been preparing to transfer to the engineering program at USC by taking university courses. Since I believe this is a goal that promotes his well-being, I share in his desire. This desire also led me to action by helping him in some practical ways. When he recently found out he got accepted to USC, I shared in his joy. His joy was my joy because I care about the good (and bad) things that happen to him as if they were happening to me. This is what love does—we are united with the loved one in desiring their good.

In addition to seeking understanding of the other and sharing his or her goals, loving connection involves emotional presence. We've all had the experience of being physically present but not emotionally present—not attending on an emotional level. We intuitively feel that this experience is lacking something. We naturally desire a deeper form of engagement in which both parties "feel felt," as psychiatrist Daniel Siegel puts it.[6] We want to know that we've impacted the other. Emotional presence requires certain ways of being with the other.

Loving connection also includes sharing intentions. When I get together with a few of my close friends and we experience a genuine connection with each other, part of this is the sharing of intentions. We share a general intention to connect with each other and promote true dialogue and understanding. This shared intention is an important aspect of emotional presence. In and through our conversation, we sense our shared intention as we check in with each other, respond with empathy and encouragement, and ask thoughtful questions.

Likewise, in psychotherapy there is a similar shared intention—at least when there is a good relationship between therapist and client. With all my clients, my overarching intention is to help them heal, grow, and feel understood. Most clients share this general intention as well, and this is the basis for a positive therapeutic relationship. There is an implicit, sometimes explicit, agreement and sense that we are working toward the same goal on a macro level (the entire therapeutic endeavor) and a micro level (any given conversation). For example, in a recent session with a client, Randy, the dialogue was deepening as we discovered how his experience of not having a voice in his family growing up was playing out in his work relationships. Randy gained new insights and felt healing emotions. Based on our shared intention, we had a shared experience of emotional presence that involved working together to help him feel known and accepted.

Beyond a cognitive connection, emotional presence also involves empathy. When I am with my close friends, we feel present with one another in love partly because we're attuned to each other's feelings. When I see on a friend's face that he "gets" what I am feeling, I have a deep sense of emotional presence. In this sharing of affect, there is a union that is part of the very essence of love. Likewise in psychotherapy, emotional attunement is a core aspect of helping clients feel that their therapist is emotionally present and not just going through the motions.

There is also a sense of mutual closeness with close friends— another aspect of loving connection. Though we talk about current events and catch up on our daily lives, we also share things that are important to us—things that reveal who we are and who we want to become. We share triumphs, struggles, and desires with respect to our work, colleagues, friends, and family. This requires a level of vulnerability, so there is an emotional risk involved. What if the others don't respond well? What if they don't understand or judge me?

Even with close friends I sometimes hear the faint whisper of these anxieties. I suspect many of us feel this way at times. Yet, on the other side of this risk is the feeling of closeness; the feeling of being known, understood, accepted, and loved. This happens when we deliberately share our internal world, allowing our friend the privilege of seeing our soul. This invites reciprocation and creates a sense of mutual closeness.

THE ART OF LOVE

Responding to others in love requires responsiveness to their particular personalities, needs, and the situation. In addition, we have to be aware of how our own attachment tendencies affect our ability to be responsive. There is no formula because love is an art. On one occasion, when my younger son Aiden was a teenager, he got very mad at me for telling him something he believed wasn't true. From my perspective what I said was true, but he interpreted it too literally. I tried to explain this, but to no avail. He accused me of lying, I got offended and angry, and an argument ensued with some fairly heated yelling on both sides. I realized I needed to end the argument and cool down, so I left the room.

As I was processing what had happened, I saw that in my response I was focused on myself. I was offended that my son could think I lied to him because this made me "look bad." In the stress, my attachment tendencies triggered underlying anxiety about whether I was a good enough father. I needed to focus on Aiden's needs, an insight informed by the nature of our relationship. More specifically, what Aiden needed at that moment to promote his good and our connection was for me to initiate repair, show empathy regarding his feelings, and provide the emotional security that being trustworthy is of utmost importance to me. My assessment was based on our relationship, the situation, and his developmental level. Being responsive and able to shift my focus to his needs was based on some measure of self-awareness and internal security.

So I talked to Aiden and tried to convey these things. He took this in, and it did indeed promote his good and our connection. Love, then, needs to be responsive to the nature of a relationship, the other person's particular needs, and our own self-protection and attachment tendencies.

Lewis famously wrote about the "four loves" present in Scripture— philia, agape, eros, and storge—corresponding to friendship love, divine love, romantic love, and parental or attachment love.[7] Some have suggested that, while there is one unitary concept of love (goodwill + loving connection), there are not qualitatively different types of love but different forms. To love someone well requires that the love have an appropriate form, depending on the kind of relationship and the characteristics of the loved one. Another way of saying this is that love is an art that requires responsiveness. Love isn't generic or abstract; rather, it adapts to love each person well.[8]

In this vein, Stephen Post notes that love can take many forms, including celebration when someone demonstrates good character or a noteworthy accomplishment; active compassion when someone is suffering; forgiveness when someone needs reconciliation; care when someone is ill; companionship when someone is lonely; and correction when someone is promoting ill-being.[9] These are just a few examples, but knowing when to employ any given form of love is an art that requires responsiveness and wisdom.

There are three major factors that affect the good we seek for others and the loving connection we desire to have with others: (1) the type of relationship, (2) the characteristics and needs of the other person, and (3) self-awareness about our own self-protection tendencies based on our attachment history. Love, then, is inherently responsive to these nuances. Because of this, we can think of love as an art, a phrase used by Lewis.[10] I take it to refer to the intuitive or implicit knowledge involved in loving a person in the context of the specific relationship and in a way that's responsive to the person's particular needs at a given moment. So what does it look like for us to be responsive in these ways?

Love calls for different types of connection or unity with strangers, spouses, friends, and children, to name a few types of relationships. These various types of relationships also put boundaries around what love can look like with a particular person. It may seem like this would restrain love from its full expression. However, the nature of a relationship actually provides the very shape of its full expression, and love is informed by that shape. Instead of limiting love, relational characteristics provide the contours of love.

In our desire to connect in love, there are clear differences in our ability to gain knowledge of others depending on the type of relationship we have with them. We may exercise our love of a brother or sister in Christ in a different social group or culture solely through our understanding of what it means to be a human being. We may have no means of gaining more information about them, but on the grounds of knowing they are made in the image of God, we can understand the common need for food and shelter, for protection and provision, and for human dignity and autonomy.

My ability to gain knowledge of and achieve unity through presence and closeness with my wife, however, is quite another matter. Not only do I know her well because of our common life together, but we spend a great deal of time in conversation, enabling me to grow in my understanding of who she is and what she needs. This allows for the kind of emotional presence and mutual closeness more appropriate to this kind of relationship, and informs my loving actions on her behalf. For example, we can experience emotional presence and mutual closeness that come from co-parenting our children. When we share a common goal in the context of parenting, it promotes a certain texture of emotional presence that is deep and not possible in other more superficial relationships. When I am vulnerable and reveal to my wife things about myself as a parent, it promotes a sense of mutual closeness that's shaped by the nature of our relationship.

Like the spousal relationship, parenting has certain parameters for love built into it. We don't love our children in the same way we love our friends or spouses. Even though my sons are important to me, when they were young, I didn't reveal many aspects of my own struggles to them, because it wouldn't have been in their best interest. They wouldn't have understood, and it might have caused them to feel confused or overwhelmed. This sort of sharing is generally not appropriate in a parent-child relationship because it doesn't promote the good of the child. The essential reason for this has to do with the very nature of the relationship. Parents need to manage their own emotions so they can help manage the child's emotions in order to develop a secure attachment and the capacity to love. In contrast, I can share certain struggles with a friend or with my wife because it's appropriate within these relational contexts. The parent-child relationship precludes certain forms of mutual closeness that would be disordered and carries within it a structure for other forms of mutual closeness that promote love.

To take an extreme example, sex within the confines of a marriage relationship is appropriate and loving, but it is always a gross violation of a parent-child relationship. This is, in fact, why incest causes so much damage to a child: it violates the very nature of the relationship, and it isn't an act of love precisely because it cannot and does not promote well-being, emotional presence, or mutual closeness. On the contrary, it causes internal fragmentation in both parties, but especially in the child who is more vulnerable.

The therapist-client relationship also has certain parameters for love built into it. Though there are unique features to this relationship, there are many parallels with parenting as well. For example, the therapist may share aspects of his or her experience in order to help the client grow, but out of love the therapist won't share internal struggles to such an extent that it leaves the client feeling insecure or overwhelmed. Once again, certain forms of emotional presence and mutual closeness are not possible, but others are possible and in fact unique to a therapeutic relationship.

Friendship, likewise, impacts how we share in others' perspectives and how we experience presence and closeness with them. Friendship calls for us to be committed to the other's well-being, to share activities and experiences, and to reveal certain kinds of things that are important to us, but not in the same way as a spousal relationship. Sexual intimacy and certain types of emotional intimacy are limited, in love, to a spousal relationship. In sum, love must be responsive to the nature and form of a relationship, and there are other nuanced ways it must be responsive to the individual.

The good and loving connection we seek with another is impacted also by the characteristics and needs of the other given their overall context and development. For example, a person with an abusive background may react negatively to physical touch. I had a client, Amelia, for whom this was the case. I sometimes shake hands with clients, and very occasionally hug a client, but Amelia could not shake my hand due to her history of abuse. Over the course of numerous years of therapy she was never able to shake my hand, even though part of her wanted to do so. A form of loving presence that involves shaking hands was not possible for Amelia at that time, and so it wouldn't have been loving for me to try to engage in this form of contact.

Likewise, a loved one may have limited capacity to share attention focused on the self or self-reveal in ways that promote mutual closeness. This could be, for example, someone who is developmentally delayed and has a limited capacity to know his internal world and to self-reveal what is important to him. Regardless of our desire to be emotionally close and the appropriateness of it in the context of the relationship, his abilities may limit the connection and unity we are able to achieve. In this case we promote whatever kind of loving connection is possible for this particular person.

The examples could be endless, but the art of love is revealed in the particulars of a given situation. Each situation requires wisdom and discernment in how to love well given the relationship, the person, and the broader context. This is a process we engage in every day.

A while back, one of my students encountered a difficult relational experience with a colleague of mine in a meeting in which I was present. My response required a delicate balance to account for his needs and our relationship, my relationship with my colleague, and the department as a whole. Since I was his academic adviser, I reached out to see if he wanted to meet and process this experience. We met, and I tried to listen, validate his experience, and praise him for how he handled the situation, while at the same time not "taking sides" in order to honor my relationship with colleagues involved. I also attempted to discern what he needed, given his level of development as a graduate student in his midtwenties. I believed he needed support and empowerment, but that he needed to deal directly with the others involved without my being in the middle. He also needed to feel connected to and valued by our community, so I attempted to promote this.

Being responsive to another person's needs also requires awareness of our insecure attachment tendencies. These tendencies sometimes hinder us from providing the necessary loving response. After my argument with my son Aiden, if I had become engulfed in my anxiety, I wouldn't have been able to provide the response he needed—to communicate that it was important to me to be trustworthy. The art of love requires that we engage in a lifelong process of growing in self-awareness and internal security so that we are freed up to focus on others. We can respond to our own emotional insecurities by processing them so they don't define us and hinder our ability to love.

Love takes on many forms but has two basic components: desiring and pursuing the good of the other, and connection with the other. We find that sometimes our love falls short, even with the best of intentions. In order for our loving intentions to promote others' well-being, we must understand their unique needs. An intrinsic part of promoting others' well-being is fostering connection with others, which involves sharing life-affirming goals and emotional presence (shared intentions, empathy, and mutual closeness). The fullest expression of the good we seek for others is loving connection with God and sharing this loving connection with others.

Finally, there is no formula for love because love is an art. As such, love is responsive to the nature of a relationship, the particulars of another's needs, and our own self-protection based on our attachment tendencies. The type of relationship we have with another person places boundaries around how we can love that person. Rather than restraining love, the nature of the relationship provides the very shape of its full expression. Love, then, is never generic or abstract. As we reflect God's love to others, we strive to discern the unique and specific response that will promote the well-being of others. We also strive to work through our own emotional insecurities and barriers so we can provide the response needed at a given time. We turn now to the notion of deep love, in which we explore how to balance the competing priorities of love and what it means to love Christianly.

10

Deep Love

WE'RE CALLED to bring God's love to the world and to love those closest to us. I struggle with this in two ways. On one hand, when I look at the scope of the crises in our world—the global refugee crisis, the polarization in the United States, and the Covid-19 pandemic—I often freeze up, unable to answer the question, "What do I do?"

On the other hand, I sometimes focus on helping people "out there," or "doing good" to gain recognition, all the while neglecting those closest to me. I've done this to my family more than I care to remember. There was a time in my life when my busyness got out of control. I had served for three years in the Army as a psychologist before becoming a professor. I then decided I needed more training, so I went back to graduate school at UCLA while working full time. A lot of this was driven by my insecurities. After a few years of this crazy pace, things in my life started to come unhinged. I was doing all this good work, but at the expense of loving the people who depended on me the most.

Because all people are created in the image of God, our call to love extends to everyone. This is captured by one of the five dimensions of love identified by sociologist Pitirim Sorokin, in what he called "extensivity":

The extensivity of love ranges from the zero point of love of oneself only, up to the love of all mankind, all living creatures, and the whole universe. Between the minimal and maximal degrees lies a vast scale of extensivities: love of one's own family, or a few friends, or love of the groups one belongs to—one's own clan, tribe, nationality, nation, religious, occupational, political, and other groups and associations.[1]

The dimensions of extensivity point to the tension in balancing love for those closest to us, such as family and friends, with love for those "out there"—all of humanity and particularly the poor and marginalized of the world. Because we have limited resources, we have to constantly make choices to extend our love to some but not others.

Scripture emphasizes loving the poor and the marginalized (e.g., James 2:14-17; Galatians 2:10). Yet we also see the special importance of loving family (e.g., Ephesians 5:21-28; 6:1-4). It's possible to become out of balance on both ends of the spectrum. Some love only those in their inner circle and show little concern for people outside who are in need. But Stephen Post points out that it's also possible for someone "to be so focused on the needs of all humanity that the importance of special relationships is missed."[2] I have been guilty of this as well. How, then, do we go about balancing the competing priorities of love?

THE PRIORITIES OF LOVE

There are risks on both sides of this issue: neglecting those closest to us, and neglecting the needs of wider humanity, particularly the poor and needy within our reach.[3] As a general principle it seems prudent to start with our little corner of the world as a foundation, and extend this love where possible, which requires great wisdom in practice.[4]

Building on the right foundation for love is critical. We are embodied and relational beings; we are located in a particular place and time, and we can only extend ourselves so much. We relate most deeply to those in our daily life. We have a profound responsibility to the people we interact with day in and day out, and even more so with those who rely on us for care: our children, spouses, partners, employees, friends, coworkers, and those who are hurting in our communities. Infants, for example, rely on their parents to literally regulate their emotions through eye contact and nonverbal communication.

These early attachment experiences shape the very structures of our sense of self and affect every aspect of development. Furthermore, parents as attachment figures are not replaceable in providing for the emotional needs of their child. When parental attachment figures abandon a child, it causes emotional trauma that has lifelong and far-reaching effects for that child. When parental love is closer to the ideal, it promotes secure attachment, which is a foundational component of love. Although we can't develop full attachment relationships with everyone, this is the type of love we seek to extend outside ourselves.

In fact, attachment relationships may be the prototype of love. The parent-child love between God the Father and God the Son is held up as a model for our love of others, and we are similarly encouraged to relate to God as our "Abba," the most intimate of designations for a father. The story known as the parable of the prodigal son dramatically illustrates God's love in the form of a father's love. In addition, we'll explore in chapter fourteen our relationships with others in the church as those of a family. From a psychological perspective, we learn to love in the context of our closest attachment relationships. Our later ability to love is generalized from these first patterns. Our earliest years establish attachment filters that endure throughout life. Parental love is characterized by the "sustained emotional tendency toward the good of another that is almost always replete with helping behaviors,"[5] and results in secure attachment filters and the ability to love well. Often sacrificial in nature, it's the most intense and abiding love we know.

There is some fascinating research that supports this idea that extensive love is rooted in deep attachment love. Samuel and Pearl Oliner

interviewed over seven hundred people who lived in Nazi-occupied
Europe, including those who rescued Jews, those who chose not to
rescue Jews, and Jewish survivors.[6] In contrast to the nonrescuers, the
rescuers exhibited a deep sense of relatedness. The Oliners note:

> What distinguished rescuers was not their lack of concern with self,
> external approval, or achievement, but rather their capacity for ex-
> tensive relationships—their stronger sense of attachment to others
> and their feeling of responsibility for the welfare of others, including
> those outside their immediate familial or communal circles.[7]

This deep sense of relatedness developed during childhood. For both
rescuers and nonrescuers, their early family lives revealed that their
"respective wartime behaviors grew out of their general patterns of relating to others."[8] Rescuers generally experienced strong and cohesive
family bonds during childhood, whereas nonrescuers more often reported poor family relationships. For those who risked their lives to
rescue Jews, extended love started with attachment love in the family.

This has important implications for how we address the priorities
of love in our lives. While the risk of neglecting those closest to us
may be less than that of neglecting the needy and poor, it's nonetheless
possible—especially for those heavily involved in service. When we
invest in loving our children and those under our care in special ways,
this has a ripple effect in preparing them to extend a deep love to
others. The rescuers in the Oliners' study wouldn't have been emotionally and psychologically equipped to engage in bold acts of love
had they not received and internalized attachment love from their
parents and families. It's important to be mindful of the deep ramifi-
cations of our responsibilities to love those closest to us.

Attachment figures are irreplaceable in the psychological and emotional economy of the child. Providing occasional financial resources
and emotional support for an abandoned child doesn't take the place
of a lost attachment figure. This is a weighty responsibility for those
entrusted to care in this way. Because of this psychological reality,

which reflects God's relational design of human beings, I resonate with Stephen Post in noting that "It is reasonable to first meet the genuine needs of those closest to us for whom we are particularly responsible, for example, as parents."[9]

This, however, doesn't negate our current responsibility to extend love to broader humanity, especially the needy and the poor. This is perhaps the greater risk for most people; it's easy to become complacent by focusing on our inner circle, treating all others as outsiders. This is not an either-or situation. Instead, we must live in the tension between loving our corner of the world and extending love to the broader world. Attachment love is the basis for the capacities of a broader universal compassion. We must extend this basis by reaching out beyond those who are near and dear with an attachment-type love that represents and embodies the very love of God. We can't be a parent to everyone, but we seek to extend this quality of love to the family of God and to all people.

Christians extend attachment love to build the new family of God (more on this in chapter fourteen). Adoption provides a theologically rich picture not only of salvation, but also of extending this intimate family-based love to those beyond our immediate biological family in forming the new family of God. Through faith in Christ we are adopted as sons and daughters of God and into the family of God (Romans 8:15, 23; 9:4; Galatians 4:5; Ephesians 1:5). People who were formerly outside the family based on biological lines become part of a new family of God.

The concept of family and the attachment-type love entailed in family described a new reality for first-century Christians. This new, radically re-envisioned family crossed socioeconomic, cultural, and ethnic lines in order to show God's character of love more clearly. The new family of God was designed to be a society that contrasted with society-at-large by living out a new social order of love.[10] So when we wrestle with extending attachment love beyond our immediate bio-logical family, we must first redefine what family means within a new kingdom reality. Our brothers and sisters in Christ *are* family, every bit as much as our biological children and parents. While this doesn't eliminate tension between responsibilities to our biological family on the one hand and believers who are part of our local church and the universal church on the other, this reality should inform how we wrestle with the tensions and balance our love.

Beyond the family of God, and especially those in our local fellowship, we face tensions in how to extend love to all of humanity, particularly the poor and marginalized. In 1963, Suzie Valadez moved to El Paso, Texas to care for the impoverished Mexican people living in the Ciudad Juarez garbage dump.[11] Despite being a single mother of four with very little money, she followed her calling and provided religious services, food, and clothing for the people of Ciudad Juarez. Over time, she became known as the "Queen of the Dump" and attracted help for her cause from various foundations, business leaders, and volunteers. She has been noted as a moral exemplar for her work.[12] Due to her work, her children were required to make very real sacri-fices, growing up with little more than the basic necessities. How do we evaluate such situations in light of the priorities of love?

Every situation is different and there are no formulas for discerning the best way to prioritize our love in any given situation. We have to consider our responsibilities before God, and seek the guidance of the Holy Spirit and wisdom. I would note that Jesus strongly emphasized caring for the poor, the widow, and the outsider. We can follow suit knowing this will often require sacrifice that isn't sanctioned by our secular culture. At the same time, how we treat those closest to us and how they experience relationship with us matters greatly.

It's possible for Valadez, for example, to approach the sacrifice nec-essary for her children in a deeply loving way that engenders closeness to her and simultaneously models an ethic of service. On the other hand, it's possible for her to have little compassion for her children's experience of sacrifice, and to ignore their developmental needs for emotional connection and support. This could cause her children harm even as she promotes the well-being of those living in the garbage dump. This latter case presents a tension that we shouldn't ignore. Instead, we need to fully experience this tension and seek wisdom as we navigate it. Stephen Post suggests that "Christian spouses and their children must be brought into greater intimacy through the spiritual harmony of purpose that emerges from the challenges of serving the world."[13]

Children can be included in our service in a way that is integrated with the family of God, creating a holistic dynamic that both promotes the well-being of the children and those the family serves. At the end of the day, we seek to love those in the new family of God with an attachment-type love, and to wisely extend this love to all people, especially the poor and needy. As we do this, our love is transformed into a deeper love that is infused by God's love.

LOVING CHRISTIANLY

When I was in the Army, there were clients I had to see as part of my job even if they were difficult or unpleasant. Mark was referred by his commander due to difficulty getting along with his fellow soldiers; I quickly saw why. The first time he walked into my office, he said, "Wow, life's been good, huh Doc?"—apparently a reference to my youthful appearance, which he clearly associated with inexperience.

Mark was condescending. He constantly criticized his coworkers and as a result he had alienated himself from all of them. Similarly, Mark picked apart my statements, challenged my knowledge, and made it clear that not only did he not need therapy, he was my moral and intellectual superior. Needless to say, I didn't look forward to my weekly sessions with Mark, and I found it difficult to desire to promote his well-being.

It's relatively easy to love others when they are lovable—attractive, pleasant, and grateful. But what about when people are difficult, entitled, and difficult to love? This raises a question: Is "Christian" love somehow different from what we might call "natural love"? In other words, should following Jesus make our love different, in general, from those who are not following Christ? Should my love for Mark in the context of therapy look different because I'm a Christian?

The answer to this is both yes and no. Following Jesus should make the love of believers different and distinct from nonbelievers. This is not to say, however, that "Christian love" is a special type of love. Rather, all forms of our love in all situations and relationships should be infused with God's love, and thereby transformed into what C. S. Lewis calls "charity."[14] Christian love is always done for the glory of the Father, in the name of Jesus, and by the power of the Holy Spirit, reflecting what we might call a trinitarian love. Christian love isn't a type of class of love; rather, it's a certain quality that permeates all forms of love in which our love is "in Christ" and reflects our abiding in Christ. Trinitarian love means that we love others as a participation in God's love.

When we approach loving others in this way, according to 1 John, our love comes from God, expresses to others who God is, and ultimately is a form of loving God. In this way, Christian love is a participation in God's love. As we participate in God's love, our natural human love retains its essential character but is elevated to something beyond itself by God who is Love. Lewis describes this transformation of natural love into "charity" in this way: "The Divine Love doesn't substitute itself for the natural—as if we had to throw away our silver to make room for gold. The natural loves are summoned to become modes of Charity while also remaining the natural loves they were."[15]

Although all of our natural love is thus transformed, Lewis emphasized the transformation of what he called "Gift-love" and "Need-love," the two correlative sides of attachment love. Gift-love corresponds to the care-giving love of a parent, and Need-love is parallel to the care-receiving love of a child. This echoes the suggestion that attachment love provides a prototype of love. As God enables divine Gift-love, we increasingly desire "what is simply best for the beloved."[16] While *natural* Gift-love is directed toward things that are intrinsically lovable, *divine* Gift-love enables us to love what is not naturally lovable—both in action and in general character. While my Gift-love for Mark was by no means perfect, I do believe that God's love helped me to persevere with his prickly exterior so I could empathize with a deeply hurting man, created in the image of God and worthy of my love, attention, and care.

Lewis notes that God also enables Gift-love toward himself. God doesn't need our love in order to be complete, but he desires our love because it is in our best interest to freely reflect God's love back to him. We offer Gift-love to God, then, by freely and joyously giving our hearts to God even as our hearts are infused with and empowered by the very same God to whom we offer our love. In addition, we offer Gift-love to God when we feed and clothe the stranger on God's behalf.

God also grants us a transformed, or supernatural, Need-love of God and others. First, with respect to our Need-love of God, Lewis contends that our natural tendency is to believe, somewhere deep down, that we don't really need God in the most basic way. We cover this up by thinking that God loves us, "not because he is Love, but because we are intrinsically lovable."[17] We *are* all worthy of love, but I don't think that is what Lewis means here. At the core, he's getting at the deeply warped sense we sometimes have that we're actually earning our salvation. *I think I can actually meet God's standards on my own; I think I've got this*, we sometimes tell ourselves. I mentioned that in my young adulthood there was a period when I approached my spirituality through knowledge and effort. I thought if I just tried hard enough and gained enough head knowledge, then God would accept me. When trials come, my first instinct is still to revert to those ways. It takes constant intentionality and internal work to allow myself to need God.

Even as we grow out of this belief, a subtler version of it takes hold. "Beaten out of this," Lewis suggests, "we next offer our own humility to God's admiration. Surely He'll like *that?* Or if not that, our clear-sighted and humble recognition that we still lack humility."[18] We can all recognize the contours of these natural tendencies at work in our hearts. In Christian Need-love, God's transforming work in our hearts enables us to gradually gain the ability to fully accept our dependence on God and others. In place of our natural Need-love, "Grace substitutes a full, childlike and delighted acceptance of our Need, a joy in total dependence."[19] In our heavenly moments, we don't seek to earn God's favor; rather, we delight in our need as our hearts declare, "God, I need you. Period."

With respect to our Need-love for others, our natural tendency is to want to be loved for that which is good in us—our strengths, beauty, skill, and virtue. To be loved in the very midst of our unloveliness makes us vulnerable. This love, while healing, also stings—it's like putting alcohol on an open wound. It disinfects and heals, but it hurts at the same time. It can be scary and difficult to receive love when we're vulnerable. It's one of the great paradoxes of life that when we are most in need of love, we are the least capable of taking it in.

There have been too many times when I have been vulnerable and hurting and pushed people away, especially those closest to me. If the good in me isn't on display and someone loves me in that, I have to face those parts of myself that I don't like. I'm often on the other side of this as well, sometimes with family members or with students and clients, and it always grieves me.

A number of years ago, a student of mine, Kay, was struggling. She had become depressed and was performing poorly in her course work and clinical work, which I was supervising. I reached out to Kay to provide support and guidance, but she declined to meet with me. The more she struggled, the more guarded she became. It was difficult for her to risk being loved in the midst of her struggles and vulnerabilities. This was her natural tendency with Need-love, and also ours.

We all have wounds, and this Need-love dynamic is heightened for those who have been consistently wounded by others in their vulnerability. This is where psychotherapy can play a pivotal role, not only in healing, but also in the transformation of natural love into Christian love or charity. In fact, this is the emotional space that much of psychotherapy focuses on—helping people receive love even when they are vulnerable. Part of how our love is transformed as Christians is that we become more able to fully and joyfully receive the caregiving love of others. Reflecting on the transformation of our love into Christian love, or charity, leads us to the question: How does this process happen?

As we participate in the love among the Trinity, our love is transformed in three interrelated ways: God's love is the reason, model, and source for the transformation of our natural love into Christian love or charity. This infusion of God's love into our love captures the notion of grace-filled love—charity (*caritas*)—that goes beyond what feels good to us in the moment. This is what the New Testament authors developed in co-opting the Greek word *agape* to represent Christian love. To the ancient Greeks, *agape* carried the idea of a love that transcends immediate emotions and reflects a higher order principle by which we deliberately live.[20] While our love shares a common core with those not following Christ, it should be different in these three ways.

First, participating in the love within the Trinity should give us a more profound *reason and motivation* to love others. We see examples of this in believers who forgive and seek the good of people who have seriously harmed them. Frank and Elizabeth Morris lost their only son when a drunk teenager, Tommy, plowed into his car two days before Christmas. Elizabeth began visiting Tommy in prison and found her hatred of him softening into compassion. Frank, a part-time preacher, ended up baptizing Tommy. Frank recounted the scene in an interview: "About 10 that night we stopped at the Little River Church. Tommy put on a baptismal gown, and I baptized him by immersion. He thanked me and asked if I'd forgive him for what he'd done. I said, 'Yes, I'll forgive you.'" They now attend church together, and most Sundays Frank and Elizabeth take Tommy out to eat.[21]

The reason for our love is that God first loved us when we didn't deserve it, as Paul tells us in Romans: "But God showed his great love for us by sending Christ to die for us while were still sinners" (Romans 5:8). This is the deepest reason a human being could possibly have to love another person. The reason for our love was enacted in the paradigmatic and most powerful story ever lived out—Jesus dying on the cross for our sins. We participate in God's love when we accept God's gift and experience the forgiveness of our sins, which in turn empowers us to love beyond our natural love and beyond a utilitarian exchange. God's love within us motivates us to offer Gift-love to others even when they behave in ways that make it difficult to love them. Undergirding this is the humility required to remember that we are also difficult to love at times.

We are meaning-making beings, and without Christ we are limited to loving in a way that makes sense within the confines of life and our natural tendencies. However, participating in the love of the Trinity expands the possibilities for our love. In Christ, our love is no longer limited by the gain we can receive, or by natural attractiveness or loveliness. Our love is also no longer limited to making sense in the world's terms or the terms of our fallen psychological processes. Christian love provides the energy for action to love beyond reason and beyond the short term. Our love is empowered by that which makes sense in the economy of the kingdom of God—the grand salvation story that connects us to God's love. This makes Christian love different.

Second, this motivation stems in part from the *model* of Jesus' love. The difference in our love is tied to the specific person of Jesus, who is God incarnate. In all he did, Jesus sought to promote the well-being of others, and he sought union or connection with others. In addition, he gave his life to make union with God possible, which is our greatest good. In Jesus, we have the ultimate model of love that transforms our natural love into a heavenly realm.

Finally, God's love is also the *source* of our love, and therefore the source of the transformation of our natural love into charity. Alexander Pruss says that this deepening of our natural love is only possible "in grace."[22] God as the source of Christian love is implicit throughout Lewis's discussion as well. For example, he notes that when people are receiving charity, they are loved because "Love Himself" is in those who love them.[23] Jesus loved others with the very same love he shared with the Father: "I have loved you even as the Father has loved me. Remain in my love" (John 15:9). Jesus invites us to abide in his love, which is a sharing or participation in the love between the Father and Son. Divine love, then, is the source of our love. We pass on the very love of God that lives within us. It is a power—or Person—within us that elevates our natural love to a heavenly love.

The implication of all of this for growing in love—which is connection and spiritual transformation—is that we need to engage in spiritual disciplines that train us to: (1) access God's forgiveness and our subsequent gratitude as deep motivation for love; (2) gain a deeper understanding and appreciation of Jesus' love for others as a model for our love; and (3) cultivate an awareness of the Holy Spirit who guides our thoughts and actions with the very love of the Trinity. May our love be more and more transformed by the love of the Trinity until that day when all our love will be worthy of heaven.

As we seek wisdom in balancing the demands of love with our limited resources, we strive to *love Christianly*; that is, to infuse our love with God's love. The New Testament depicts the love between the Father and Son, and by implication the love among all three members of the Trinity, as the reason, model, and source for our love. This provides the divine motivation to delight in others and to love beyond reason, immediate gain, and what makes sense in the short-term economy of this life. Simply put, we love because God first loved us with an extraordinary, intimate, and sacrificial love. Our experience of this love and gratitude for it fuels a divine dynamic in our love. As we share in God's love, often through the body of Christ, it becomes our own and we then pass it on to others in a positive spiral of love. We share God's love foundationally within the body of Christ and extend this family love to the world. As we do this, the love of individual believers adds up to something greater than the sum of its parts—a mutual sharing in God's loving presence, which reflects the image and glory of God. With love as our goal, we turn now to how the deep growth process works.

11

Understanding
Deep Growth

JILL HAD DECIDED to go into ministry in her late twenties. She was a natural leader and effective in her early ministry roles, but struggles were emerging. Several romantic relationships had crashed and burned, and she was experiencing conflict and distance with some of her close friends. She also felt distant from God. My work with Jill in therapy illustrates a fundamental principle regarding how spiritual and emotional growth work.

In our work together, I learned that Jill's father was often harsh and also extremely neglectful. Her mother provided some practical support, but was very anxious and had difficulty attending to Jill's emotional needs. Jill was basically left to raise herself emotionally. An articulate child, she tried expressing her emotional needs to her parents. Her needs were often dismissed, especially by her dad, who seemed to have very little capacity to deal with feelings and attend to Jill's need for secure attachment. This was painful for her given her acute awareness that she needed something more from her parents.

All of this led to an anxious (preoccupied) attachment filter in which Jill felt defective, invisible, and unworthy of people's love and care. She was often anxious, especially in relationships with authority figures. This was her mind's strategic way of protecting herself. Her attachment system was in overdrive in order to be on the lookout for rejection because, at a gut level, she expected it.

Jill would often begin to feel anxiety and a sense of shame at the first sign of withdrawal from others in her life. To cope with this, she would relentlessly try to talk things through with her friends—and often blame others—hoping to get rid of the feelings of shame. Instead, she typically overwhelmed others with her needs, leading to some form of rejection that reinforced her sense of shame. This sometimes led to a downward spiral into depression and extreme bouts of anxiety.

Jill and I processed these core issues in the beginning of therapy. She read books about growth, reached out to some friends, and got involved in a small group at her church. There were initial incremental changes that were encouraging. We gradually developed a bond, and she began to feel understood by me. She started dating a young man named Travis, and things were going well. She was better able to cope with relational ruptures, and her anxiety seemed to become less debilitating and chronic. And then she hit a wall.

The pattern of feeling that she was defective at the core and not worthy of love, seemed to come back even more strongly than before. She and Travis began having more serious struggles and conflict that would end in a downward spiral of shame and depression. Jill was putting in the work of therapy, processing painful experiences, and staying involved at her church, and yet nothing seemed to be changing during this phase. We often talked about the same patterns that were coming up, week after week.

During this time, Jill grew discouraged and wondered if she would ever feel whole, truly accepted and loved, and close to God. She would often ask, "Will things ever change for me?" and "How long will this take?" During this period, Jill would often come in and say she thought maybe it was time to stop therapy. Nothing was changing, so what was the point? For months, she was on the brink of quitting therapy. For months, I felt like I was talking her off of the ledge of despair. At times, I had my own doubts. Would Jill ever feel differently about herself at the core? Was therapy helping at all? I certainly couldn't predict exactly how or when things were going to change for Jill.

Like Jill, we all want to see immediate and clear results of our efforts to heal and grow. When we put two units of effort in, we want to see at least two units of growth immediately. When this doesn't happen—which is much of the time—it leaves us feeling helpless. And even after we do start to see some initial growth, as Jill did, we eventually hit a wall in which deeply ingrained patterns seem to persist, even if they show up in different ways. Why does this happen? Why don't we see the growth and change we expect (and maybe feel we deserve)? And when this happens, how do we stay motivated to grow? What steps do we take to keep moving forward?

THE NATURE OF DEEP GROWTH

To address these questions and struggles, the first step is to understand how deep growth works.[1] We have to see the big picture that growth is not a straight path or a solo journey; it's a winding journey filled with curves, confusing roundabouts, and seeming dead-ends. You just have to keep moving, even when the path twists and turns and you're not exactly sure where you're headed. You have to keep engaging in spiritual practices, and keep doing the internal work with the help of mentors, even when you don't see the results.

Though difficult to see, incremental changes are important and build on each other until they coalesce into something qualitatively new. When this occurs, there is a transformation in the internal landscape of our soul. Our attachment filters reorganize, leading to a new experience of the self and new ways of relating. There may be long periods of time in which small changes build on each other below the surface. We're not able to clearly see them, which can be discouraging.

At a certain point, however, one of those incremental changes will cause our attachment filters to shift. This is what we might call a "spiritual tipping point"—the moment when deep change occurs and becomes visible. A tipping point is when a small input has a large and unpredictable effect. Tipping points are an example of what scientists call "nonlinear" or "discontinuous" change.[2] These are drawn from nonlinear dynamic systems theory, which applies systems thinking to the way organisms change and develop. Even though deep growth is a winding journey, if we keep doing the work with the help of fellow travelers and God, we'll find our bearings and see growth over the long haul.

Despite Jill's despair, somewhere deep down I had faith that our relational connection was growing deeper roots, and that this was preparing the way for change. I just didn't know how, and I couldn't predict when we would see deep growth take hold. I persisted week after week trying to attune to Jill's emotions and help her feel that I was with her in this journey. Jill also persisted in spiritual practices and in doing the difficult internal work of facing painful issues week after week. We kept plugging away through the difficult "working through" phase of therapy.

Then at one point in the therapy, seemingly out of the blue, a tipping point occurred. In a way, nothing had changed in the way we worked together. There was no dramatic event that happened, and we had been talking about the same issues every week. But (seemingly) all of a sudden, over a period of several months, I noticed that she was different. She still struggled, but Jill had changed. She felt differently about herself—more secure and confident—in a very meaningful way. Her gut-level expectations of others had shifted. She felt more secure in my care for her; she began to truly trust and really feel that I was *for* her. A positive shift also occurred in her relationship with Travis. She began to feel less shame and to be more present in their interactions. The walls had come down substantially, and she began to experience more meaningful connections with people and with God.

You may have experienced this kind of internal shift in yourself or witnessed it in others. We move through our daily lives, and then in the midst of a deep connection with a friend, a time of quiet prayer, or communal worship, the internal landscape of our soul shifts. It may be a small input, but it leads to a big change—deep growth that affects our core sense of self.

How, then, do these transformational shifts in our attachment filters take place, and how do we promote this kind of growth? While relationships are the vehicle for change, they are somewhat out of our control; we can't control how God and others engage with us. But there are some things that are in our control. We can do our part to facilitate the internal and relational *processes* that lead to deep growth. One of the key processes in deep growth is the integration of the two ways of knowing, facilitated by story. We'll unpack these processes and then turn in chapter twelve to key *practices* that cultivate deep growth.

THE ENGINE OF DEEP GROWTH: STORY AND THE KNOWLEDGE SPIRAL

A key process in deep growth is bringing together the two ways of knowing—explicit knowledge and implicit relational knowledge—so they work together in harmony. In this integrating, back-and-forth process, we create and discover meaning through a story process. This happens in two ways, although in reality they're both part of one overall dynamic process of reorganizing our experiences and knowledge. In one dimension, we *interpret our own experience* through telling our story to ourselves and others. In another dimension, we *feel an idea* as we hear stories that work explicit knowledge into our hearts. Both of these micro-story processes are part of the knowledge spiral and both go through four phases with different starting points. Wilma Bucci described the way in which the two types of knowledge integrate in the context of the scientific discovery process. She delineated this with the four phases of *preparation, incubation, illumination, and interpretation.* These phases also apply to the emotional discovery process and transformational change.[3]

In explaining the way story unifies ideas and emotion, screenwriter Robert McKee provides a helpful vantage point on the knowledge spiral, which he refers to as the process of *reorganization*. He states: "Your intellectual life prepares you for emotional experiences that then urge you toward fresh perceptions that in turn remix the chemistry of new encounters."[4] Regardless of where you start in the process, each way of knowing mutually shapes and informs the other. Let's consider the knowledge spiral from the perspective of both starting points: interpreting our experience and feeling an idea.

INTERPRETING OUR EXPERIENCE

Previously I mentioned the concept of *unthought knowns* as a picture of our relational way of knowing.[5] These are things we know, yet they remain unthought and unformed; they are emotional meanings that don't exist in words that can be communicated to others. This is part of why changing our attachment filters is so profoundly difficult.[6] The very nature of our attachment filters is that they are *unspeakable*, and when they're painful it's even more difficult to be aware of and communicate them to others. When they remain unspeakable, they're very difficult to transform because they don't come into relational contact with God or others to bring new emotional information to bear on them. Our unthought knowns can become speakable, however, through a translation process that links our raw, implicit knowledge with words and ideas. This translation happens through the process of telling our story, which involves the four phases mentioned above.

A fascinating thing about narratives is that telling coherent stories about our experiences requires a harmonious working relationship between the right and left sides of the brain, and between the two ways of knowing. The "interpretive" left side of the brain is predominantly responsible for recounting the logical sequence of events, whereas the right side is predominantly responsible for the emotional meaning of the events.[7] When both of these ways of knowing are working together, you get a logical *and* emotionally meaningful, or coherent, communication of a person's sense of self.

I'll illustrate this process with my client, Jake, who lost his mother in a car accident when he was young. During the beginning of therapy, he held a deep, unarticulated experience of anger toward his father for not helping him process the loss of his mother. The *preparation* for this experience to be interpreted and transformed involved the ongoing work of therapy. Jake experienced resonance and attunement from me, and gradually became attached to me, preparing him to feel safe enough (through an internal secure base) to begin to feel anger at his father, despite the risk of loss. The preparation phase can also involve explicit knowledge or ideas that shape our experiences. Jake had read quite a bit about loss, grief, and psychological growth. This knowledge didn't directly change his experience, but it was part of the preparation that facilitated a richer experience of our relationship and work together. We'll return to this idea.

All of this prepared the way for Jake to begin to *incubate* his inchoate experience of anger toward his father. In the incubation phase, we continue to reflect on our experiences in the background of our mind and soul. Our implicit knowledge system processes our relational experiences and filters—our sense of connection and expectations in relationships. The rules that govern this processing are not known, and all this happens behind the scenes, outside of our awareness. This is the place where we form new connections about the meaning of our experiences, about our sense of self-in-relation to others. It is the place where new story lines are forged.

At the beginning of therapy, Jake didn't feel consciously angry toward his father, but when the subject of how his father handled the loss came up, he would become visibly uncomfortable and change the subject. Gradually, he began reflecting on this experience in the back of his mind. He began bringing it up on occasion in our sessions. Through our discussions, stronger emotions emerged, but they were still difficult to define.

This morphed seamlessly into the *illumination* phase, in which Jake transitioned from a vague sense of discomfort about how his father handled his loss to a more focused feeling of irritation and confusion. In illumination, the connections forged in the incubation phase make themselves known, as if coming from the outside. In the context of transforming our attachment filters and capacity to love, illumination is the tipping point in which new gut-level meanings about ourselves, God, and others are crystalized. These new meanings, or attachment filters, may have existed in a nascent form, but now they come into more clear focus in our conscious awareness. Jake became increasingly aware of feelings of anger toward his father and the need for distance. These feelings were there in the background, but now they became clearer and more conscious. This led to a stronger sense of self as he became more his own person, less defined by his father's need to avoid loss. These feelings became a focus of our work for a significant period of time during the illumination phase.

This moved into the next phase, *interpretation*, in which Jake began to interpret these new implicit experiences by translating them into words and ultimately into his story. Here we give shape and form to the illuminations, which gives us more access to the implicit meanings within ourselves. *The very process of interpreting our experience transforms it.* In this phase, Jake was able to capture his experiences more precisely in words. For example, at one point he told me, "I needed my dad's support as a child, but he let me down by making it unsafe to talk about our loss." This interpretive process enabled him to see the overall impact this had on his life and to feel not just anger toward his dad, but also a new sense that is was okay to feel angry. This is part of how interpreting his previously inchoate experience changed the experience. It was now much more defined, and it led to a new overall experience of self that his feelings are okay, and that he is worth loving. This ultimately led to a growing forgiveness of his father and a new sense of security with God.

The point of all this is that part of working toward spiritual growth is telling your story about your important relationships to significant people in your life. When you do this, two things happen that facilitate the spiritual transformation process. First, telling your story is like working a muscle. Although your story may not be totally coherent, the act of narrating your relational experiences causes the two hemispheres of the brain to work together. Second, telling your story makes your implicit experiences explicit and brings them into contact with God and others. This allows more deliberative processing to transform the experiences. The very act of narrating your experiences changes your perception of the experiences, allowing them to provide a loving connection that will bring growth and healing.

FEELING AN IDEA: AESTHETIC EMOTION

The second way the two ways of knowing come together through story is when we "feel an idea"—a concept noted in chapter five.[8] Through story, an idea or meaning becomes fused with our emotions and implicit knowledge, thus transforming it. How does story change us? It does so by conveying explicit knowledge in the implicit realm through the structure embedded within it.

Robert McKee tells us, "The exchange between artist and audience expresses ideas directly through the senses and perceptions, intuition and emotion."[9] Story doesn't explain its view of life, its explicit knowledge, in abstract ideas. Instead it creates what McKee calls "aesthetic emotion"—the feeling of an idea. This is a more structured form of implicit knowledge—a knowing that exists in our emotions and experience but carries within it an idea. Aesthetic emotion is a very important concept because it exists at the borderline between implicit and explicit knowledge, coming very close to a fusion between the two.

Stories carry knowledge within them, housed in the very structure of the sequence of events and the experiences we live through vicariously. Regardless of genre, the idea or meaning of a story is expressed or dramatized in the emotionally charged story *climax*. The hero comes to a moment of decisive choice—a true dilemma—at the story's climax. The hero's choice at the climax reveals the controlling idea of the story. Movies communicate ideas directly through the medium of visual story. You see an idea played out in the structure of the events that occur. More specifically, you feel the idea as you see it visually dramatized. It's a deeper and more direct form of knowledge than grasping a proposition in an intellectual sense.

For example, in the movie *Martian Child*, science fiction writer and widower, David Gordon, adopts an orphaned boy, Dennis, who thinks he's from Mars. Throughout the film, the human experience of the story is dramatized and we feel a profound idea about our own relationships: loss profoundly hinders our ability to love. After a series of relational breakthroughs and setbacks between David and Dennis, Dennis finally runs away and climbs a tower to wait for his Martian people to come take him home. David finds him, climbs the tower, and reaches out to Dennis with an emotional plea: "Dennis, you're my son, you belong to me, and I will never, ever, ever, ever, ever, ever, ever . . . leave you."[10] At this moment Dennis faces a dilemma—continue to hope that Martians will come take him home, or give up his defenses and take the risk of trusting David. As Dennis runs into David's arms, we immediately feel the controlling idea: love overcomes loss when we face our fears and reach out to one another.

The same principles apply to stories in Scripture and stories we might hear in our spiritual communities. Jesus taught truths through story to help us feel and experience them. The parable of the prodigal son is a well-known example. In this parable, we read about the son who squanders his inheritance and yet returns home and humbly seeks his father's forgiveness: "Father, I have sinned against both heaven and you, and I am no longer worthy of being called your son" (Luke 15:21). The father, who represents God, has a choice in his response: reject his son, or forgive him and welcome him back into the family. When we read that the father was filled with love and compassion when he saw his son a long way off, and then threw a party to celebrate, because his son "was dead and has now returned to life," we feel the idea: God is profoundly forgiving of us, and we should seek to emulate his forgiveness. Jesus' parables are designed to help us "feel God's truth" so we know and inhabit it in a deeper way than just intellectually.

In our spiritual communities, we often share stories of spiritual growth and faith because they, too, help us feel an idea. These "God stories" help us see what faith looks like in a real-life context and add richness to our implicit relational knowledge and faith in God. For example, recently my mother-in-law, Rosa, shared that she got a message from the daughter of a woman, Estella, who attended a Bible class for children in the slums where Rosa taught when she was a teenager. Every Sunday afternoon for six years, Rosa and two friends would go to the slums and bring children to a local storefront and teach Bible stories and encourage them. As a result of this, Estella and her family became Christians, including her parents, grandparents, two sisters, husband, and children. Her daughter is now studying to become a missionary. Hearing this story of my mother-in-law's faithful commitment to sacrifice her time, energy, and talent for these children helps our family to feel a profound truth: one of the greatest contributions we can make in God's economy is to serve others and share the good news of Jesus.

While stories help us to feel ideas and integrate them with our implicit relational knowledge, study of biblical truths and relevant topics can do the same. As I mentioned, Robert McKee contends that our "intellectual life shapes our emotional experiences, creating fresh new perceptions."[11] This process happens through the same phases in the knowledge spiral, but in a different way.

For example, we might consider the theological theme that God is relationally present with us through Christ and the Holy Spirit. In the preparation phase, we study this theme, and gain more explicit knowledge of the details of how God's relational presence is the cornerstone of the entire biblical narrative.[12] This then moves into the incubation phase, in which our mind processes this knowledge in the background, perhaps involving some form of meditation, making connections with other experiences and concepts. In contrast to the process of interpreting an experience, what is incubated here is not a raw emotional experience, but explicit knowledge. This transitions into the illumination phase, in which connections are formed regarding God's relational presence, which then shapes and impacts our experience of God. As we pray, for example, we become more aware of God's presence in the here and now because the meaning of this experience takes on new dimensions in light of the illumination from the richness of this concept throughout Scripture. This propositional truth, with the help of the Holy Spirit, begins to take root more in our heart and we begin to experience God's presence in new ways.

It's easy to neglect taking the time to sit quietly with the great truths of Scripture, yet we're repeatedly exhorted to do so in Scripture: "Whatever is true, whatever is noble, whatever is right, whatever is pure, whatever is lovely, whatever is admirable—if anything is excellent or praiseworthy—*think about* such things" (Philippians 4:8 NIV, emphasis added). With time and processing, these truths will make their way from our heads to our hearts.

Deep growth is not a straight path or a solo journey. Small, incremental changes eventually hit a tipping point, producing a seemingly sudden shift in our attachment filters and sense of self. Even when we don't feel like we're growing, it's important to stay the course—to keep putting in the effort to grow, with the help of God and others. While there are many things outside our control, there are certain things we can do to facilitate a key aspect in the growth process—the integration of the two ways of knowing. As we tell our own story and hear the stories of others, we *interpret our experiences* and *feel ideas*, both of which meld implicit and explicit knowledge into a more holistic knowledge of how to love God and others. This is how we are loved into loving. We turn now to the practices that help us cultivate deep growth.

12

Cultivating Deep Growth

THERE HAVE BEEN SIGNIFICANT PERIODS in my life when I was engaging in spiritual practices and yet still felt far away from God. There were times I felt like giving up. What was the point? Nothing seemed to help me feel closer to God or more spiritually alive.

We all face this question at different times in our lives. Do we give up striving for spiritual growth? Do we settle for just going through the motions? Or, do we continue striving to grow in our love for God and neighbor even when the journey is winding and confusing? We have to answer this question in our heart of hearts many times throughout our lives.

Dumbledore once told Harry Potter: "It is our choices, Harry, that show what we truly are, far more than our abilities."[1] There is a deep truth here. Our experiences and abilities shape us greatly, but so do our choices. We always have choice at some level. Sometimes that choice is nothing more than reaching out to someone who can help us see the forest through the trees. You can seek out someone who helps you feel understood, known, and accepted, and helps you keep going.

Athletes must make this choice every time they practice. They train to grow in their athletic abilities. They make the choice to engage in deliberate practice even though it's hard and the results don't always come immediately. But they also need coaches to help them know how to practice in an informed way. We are also training for something: to become more like Christ, and to grow in our love for God and neighbor.

Paul uses an athletic analogy in 1 Corinthians 9:24-27. In talking about giving up his rights in order to proclaim the gospel, Paul says:

> Don't you realize that in a race everyone runs, but only one person gets the prize? So run to win! All athletes are disciplined in their training. They do it to win a prize that will fade away, but we do it for an eternal prize. So I run with purpose in every step. I am not just shadowboxing. I discipline my body like an athlete, training it to do what it should. Otherwise, I fear that after preaching to others I myself might be disqualified.

While deep growth requires telling our story and an integration of the two ways of knowing, we must also intentionally engage in spiritual practices that develop our ability to love. The melding of the two ways of knowing through story is the engine of deep growth in the background, but we have to do our part to run the engine. We have to cultivate deep growth through deliberate spiritual practices that create the internal and relational conditions for growth.

DELIBERATE SPIRITUAL PRACTICE

So what is deliberate practice in general? Anders Ericsson, a psychologist who studies expertise and performance, coined the term *deliberate practice*.[2] He discovered three main factors that separate great performers from good or average performers. First, the great performers generally spend significantly more time in practice than the other two groups. Second, the type of practice top performers engage in is different—it's focused on a specific goal. Third, top performers set goals that stretch them beyond their comfort zone. They use practice methods that have been developed by masters in their field. They also get very fast feedback on what they're doing wrong so they can adjust accordingly and quickly. We can apply these principles to spiritual growth.

Dallas Willard defined discipline as "an activity within our power—something we can do—which brings us to a point where we can do what we at present cannot do by direct effort."[3] Spiritual disciplines don't directly affect our ability to love God and others. However, they affect our growth indirectly by facilitating the relational processes that bring about transformation.

Growing in our relational knowledge of how to connect and love requires a lot of practice. And it requires *deliberate* practice. We need to focus on specific outcomes that stretch us beyond our current relational knowledge and spiritual maturity level. We need to rely on methods taught in Scripture and developed by spiritual masters who are further down the road. We're blessed with many spiritual fathers and mothers who have taught spiritual disciplines throughout the history of the church. And there are contemporary spiritual mentors whose writings can serve to guide us on our journey.

The last few decades have seen a resurgence of interest in ancient spiritual practices aimed at cultivating an intimate relationship with God. For centuries prayer, lectio divina (spiritual reading of Scripture), meditation on Scripture or contemplation of God, solitude, silence, and worship have been employed to collaborate with the Holy Spirit in order to experience God's relational presence and grow in love. All of these practices have the potential to help us integrate the two ways of knowing. They pave the way for transformation by facilitating new experiences of God and others. As psychologist Eric Johnson puts it, "Christians have to re-wire their brains for accessing glory."[4]

Rather than trying to cover an exhaustive list of spiritual practices, what I want to do here is briefly highlight three key, interrelated practices. These include Scripture, contemplative prayer/mindfulness, and spiritual community. We'll cover the first two, Scripture and contemplative prayer/mindfulness, in this chapter and devote chapter fourteen to the third practice, spiritual community.

KNOWING GOD THROUGH SCRIPTURE

Reading, studying, and meditating on Scripture has been central to how Christians grow in love and character from the earliest days of Christianity.

Engaging with Scripture is clearly a foundational spiritual practice for two key reasons: (1) it helps us know about God, and (2) it helps us integrate this explicit knowledge into a knowledge of God that is relational and experiential. To know God in this way is to participate in the love among the Trinity, and this transforms us at the core of our being. Both ways of knowing are important here, and they need to be integrated in order to cultivate deep growth in our ability to love. As we engage with Scripture, we need to apply the principles of deliberate practice mentioned earlier. This involves: (1) devoting a meaningful amount of time to engaging with Scripture; (2) focusing on specific goals in our growth in Scripture engagement; and (3) identifying goals that will stretch us beyond our comfort zone in both our explicit and implicit knowledge of Scripture.

The Bible helps us know about God through explicit knowledge of its content. It provides the parameters for understanding God's grand story, which includes understanding who God is and how we ought to live. Scripture provides principles for how to live, but more broadly, it lays out an overall vision for the kind of life—eternal life—into which God is restoring us as the new humanity. A clear and poignant example of this is the Sermon on the Mount. In this well-known sermon, Jesus lays out a vision of the flourishing or virtuous life. Christians here are called *makarios*, often translated as "blessed," but which more accurately gets at the notion of flourishing, well-being, or health of the soul, as noted in chapter nine.[5] An understanding of the virtuous life of love for which we are to strive is important. The Sermon on the Mount synopsizes Scripture in presenting the flourishing life as one of integrated character that flows into selfless service and love for God and others. As we deliberately engage with Scripture, we need to stretch and grow in our understanding of the *makarios*, or flourishing life.

Engaging with Scripture is an act of faith that involves not just our head, but our heart as well. When we open its pages, we seek God. As N. T. Wright said, "The sheer activity of reading Scripture, in the conscious desire to be shaped and formed within the purposes of God, is itself an act of faith, hope, and love, an act of humility and patience."[6] Immersing ourselves in Scripture is an act of humble dependence on God. It is to acknowledge before God our need for grace, mercy, healing, correction, insight, encouragement, and strength. When we bring our whole self to Scripture, with an intentional posture of dependence, it opens a window for God to transform our implicit relational knowledge. Our knowledge *about* God becomes fused with a deeper, more integrated relational knowledge of the love with which he meets our dependence on him.

When we think about engaging with Scripture, we might wonder why we read parts of Scripture repeatedly and why our churches collectively revisit portions of Scripture. The reason is that the gospel—the good news of Jesus Christ—has unending implications for our lives. The early church fathers referred to this as the mystery, or *mystērion*, of the gospel.[7] This idea invokes the importance of implicit relational knowledge. While the conceptual knowledge base within Scripture is quite vast, although limited, the relational knowledge of God and his love cannot be exhausted. We'll spend the rest of our lives and throughout eternity searching and learning and growing in the deep knowledge of God's love.

We encounter the unending implications of the gospel through the Bible because Scripture is "alive and powerful" (Hebrews 4:12) and the Spirit meets us in new ways each time we read it. This may involve a profound intellectual understanding, but it's more than that. It is a deeper experiential, relational knowing of God, his love, and what this means for our sense of self and for the specifics of our life situation. As we engage with Scripture, we encounter God in new ways each time, and this represents and expresses our salvation anew—both individually and corporately as the body of Christ. Scripture, then, mediates the deep, inexhaustible love, mercy, and grace of God for our lives.

The Bible is a unified *story* of how God is creating a new people or family, through Jesus, to one day fully live in his presence and reflect his glory. Scripture helps us to locate our individual story and identity within God's grand story. This involves both implicit and explicit knowledge. There are principles and content in Scripture that help us understand, at a conceptual level, the nature of the kingdom of God, which is already here, but not yet fully present. This gives us an intellectual grasp of this *eternal* kind of life—life among the body of Christ in God's presence.

Yet, as I've emphasized, this kind of knowledge is not enough. The more we engage with Scripture and grasp the overarching story, the more we experience our identity as being "in Christ," a child of God, a brother or sister within the new family of God, and a co-heir with Christ. The story God is telling is much larger than our own story; it encompasses the whole of the universe and every person within it. And yet, our stories are a meaningful part of God's grand story. God's transcendent story is a mosaic of the redeeming work he is doing in every person's life and heart. Your story represents God's larger story, and in a very real way, moves the grand narrative forward. In other words, it matters that we grow and bring God's presence more and more into this life. It's within the story of Scripture that we find and form our identity—our deep sense of self as a child of God.

The Bible is not only God's grand story; it also engages with us through examples of others' faith, which have an implied story form. Stories shape our character and soul. As I noted in chapter eleven, Jesus used stories to help his hearers feel the truths he lived and embodied. New Testament writers, likewise, told stories about Jesus' encounters to help their hearers feel the ideas they were trying to get across. Jesus' parables, such as the farmer scattering seed in Matthew 13:3-9, are designed to reveal our hearts and our implicit knowledge, and to transform them by feeling an idea.

The parables focus thematically on deepening our knowledge of God and ourselves, including our need for salvation. In the parable of the lost sheep, for example, we feel God's tender love and mercy when we read that just as the shepherd rejoices over finding the lost sheep, "there is more joy in heaven over one lost sinner who repents and returns to God than over ninety-nine others who are righteous and haven't strayed away!" (Luke 15:7). In the story of the unforgiving debtor, a servant was forgiven an unimaginably large amount of money, then turned around and refused to forgive a much smaller debt owed to him (Matthew 18:21-35). When we hear this story, we can't help but see our own hearts reflected in the unforgiving debtor. We're reminded of our inclination to put limits on our forgiveness—despite being forgiven by God an unimaginable amount, freely and without limits. We can feel the idea that we should freely forgive others, out of gratitude for what God has done for us.

Stories within the Bible don't always provide direct advice on how to live or positive models to emulate. Some stories are positive and bolster our faith—such as Abraham's faith in offering his son, Isaac, as a sacrifice—and we should reflect on them. However, there are stories throughout Scripture that seem to provide negative examples (when that very same Abraham put his wife, Sarah, and God's promises at risk due to his cowardly behavior), or are unclear in their direct application to our lives (when Jesus curses the fig tree). It's important, then, to connect stories within the Bible to the overarching theme, or controlling idea, of Jesus bringing God's presence to earth and creating a new people who show forth God's glory and live in his presence. N. T. Wright notes that biblical stories are exemplary "within the overall ongoing narrative."[8] Here we find our vocation to live out our part of this grand story as royal priests and members of God's family.

We need to see and believe that the Bible is a foundational way we encounter God relationally and access his presence. The overarching theme of the Bible is God's relational presence with his people ultimately through Jesus. Consistent with this, the Bible mediates God's very presence. We need to not just grasp Scripture at an informational level through explicit knowledge; we also need to experience God's relational presence so we are transformed at the core of our being. In engaging with Scripture, we seek to develop intimacy with God, and through that, to grow in our capacity to love.

CONTEMPLATIVE PRAYER AND MINDFULNESS

The Christian practice of mindfulness, or mindful awareness, goes back centuries in the contemplative tradition.[9] We'll draw on this but also on the psychological research on mindfulness. While the secular psychological literature doesn't address the ultimate purpose of Christian contemplative practices—intimacy with God—it's helpful in describing why these practices may, in fact, result in that kind of relational intimacy.

The practice of mindful awareness has to do with focusing our attention on our direct experience in the present moment and fostering a certain orientation to our experience characterized by curiosity, openness, acceptance, and love.[10] In the Christian tradition, mindful awareness is practiced as a type of prayer focused on one's direct experience of God and Jesus through the Holy Spirit. It has to do with giving one's full, undivided attention to relating to God in a passive, non-defensive, undemanding, open way.[11] Mindful awareness is not just being aware in a general sense. It has to do with being aware of yourself in the context of your relationship with God. Furthermore, it has to do with accepting your experience via active listening and openness to the experience of God's presence.[12] Awareness and acceptance, then, are the two key characteristics of contemplative practice.

The disciplines included in the contemplative tradition play an important role in integrating the two ways of knowing. When the contemplative prayer practices are silent, imageless, and focused exclusively on being in God's presence, a bottom-up integration may be facilitated. In this careful attention to oneself in God's presence in the present moment, images, gut-level sensations, and discrete emotions may surface and ultimately find their way into ideas as we interpret our experience (as discussed in chapter eleven).

Sometimes practices in the contemplative tradition are more meditative in nature. In other words, rather than focusing only on God's presence, the focus is on a specific passage of Scripture, a visualization, or a short prayer such as the Jesus prayer: "Lord Jesus Christ, have mercy on me, a sinner." The combination of explicit knowledge with attentive meditation may result in a top-down integration of the two ways of knowing, in which explicit biblical teachings or characteristics of God find their way into implicit knowledge. Regardless of the route of the integration, practitioners of contemplative practices often report that the outcome is an awareness of being deeply loved and loving in return.[13] In fact, several recent studies on contemplative practices have reported increased perceived closeness to God with centering prayer,[14] spiritual meditation,[15] and prayer involving asking God questions, then waiting patiently and silently for a response.[16] We might say that contemplative practices facilitate a secure attachment to God. How, then, do they do this?

Mindfulness seems to cultivate awareness through silence and solitude. In our contemporary world, we're constantly bombarded with some kind of stimuli. If we don't make an intentional effort, it's easy to never be alone with our thoughts or with God. Attending to the stimuli that bombard us from the outside is precisely the opposite of mindfulness. We give up control over what we focus our attention on, and the result is that we don't attend to our own inner experience. Our attention is scattered, making it difficult for new thoughts, new information, and new perspectives to emerge. Silence and solitude help us focus our attention inward and allow new experiences to emerge.

As we practice silence, we develop the capacity to be present in the moment. The present moment is the only place we begin to be aware of our sensations, our observations of our own mind, and of a kind of knowing that has a more direct quality to it. This is a gradual process that takes intentionality, but as we develop the capacity to be mindfully aware—to be present in the moment—it leads to several beneficial outcomes: (1) we come to more easily hold multiple perspectives; (2) we become less reactive to our experiences; (3) we observe our sensations; (4) we act with a deep awareness of our own mind; (5) we label and translate our experiences in a way that doesn't remove them from their experiential nature; and (6) we don't judge our experience automatically in an autopilot mode.[17]

Numerous benefits have been demonstrated to result from the practice of mindful awareness. Mindfulness improves relationships, possibly by improving the ability to sense others' nonverbal emotional signals and internal worlds. This is likely a core mechanism of empathy, which facilitates compassion for others. In fact, research has shown that mindfulness and secure attachment are related. The two dispositions have related neurological correlates, foster similar positive psychosocial outcomes, and may mutually influence each other.[18] Mindfulness practices have been found to decrease insecure attachment, perhaps by allowing for better emotional self-regulation and by decreasing defensiveness during conflict.[19] Put simply, these practices help us love others better.

Research has shown that a specific brain circuit is activated during mindfulness (the middle prefrontal cortex) and seems to be the mechanism for all of these positive outcomes. This brain circuit provides an *integrative* function. The fibers from this area of the brain reach out and connect to distant areas of the brain, linking them to provide a functional unity. Areas that have their own special function come to function as a whole in combination with other areas. Neural integration involves tracking and influencing the neural firing patterns of various distinct regions of the brain so that they work together as a unified whole.[20] These elements remain differentiated, but they now work together as one unit, able to accomplish things they couldn't accomplish by themselves.

This type of neural integration and coordination within the brain is actually an outcome of attuned relationships. This goes back to how

God created us to connect. Secure, attuned relationships and being present in the moment in those relationships actually lay down the neural circuitry in our brains. Integration in the brain, in general, turns out to be a fundamental process in all aspects of well-being. This notion of differentiated components functioning as one unit captures a core truth at many levels of reality: the brain, the self, relationships, families, communities, and organizations of all types require integration for health and well-being. In fact, it may be that this aspect of our functioning reflects something of the trinitarian nature of God. We can think of the sharing of divine love among the Trinity (captured by the Greek word *perichōrēsis)* as the prototype of integration.

One of the mechanisms involved in mindfulness helps us understand the positive outcomes it brings about. Richard Davidson has shown that mindfulness helps people regulate their emotions by approaching them.[21] He found that when people encounter emotion-provoking stimuli, it activates a part of the brain (left anterior prefrontal area) that is believed to be associated with positive emotions and with approach. It appears, then, that being present in the moment and being mindful of our own mind helps us to approach our emotions with a positive stance—perhaps one of curiosity and acceptance. This in turn helps us to regulate our emotions and understand their meaning. This is likely a fundamental process involved in integrating the two ways of knowing.

Being present in the moment is a core part of what it means to find our identity in Christ and to express this identity through service, rather than finding our identity in the "doing" of our service.[22] In other words, mindful awareness is central to help our doing flow from our being. Only when we are present in the moment can our doing flow from our being. If we're not present in the moment, we operate on automatic pilot, and there is little sense of being. Doing is operating on its own, apart from any conscious, attending "I," and apart from the Holy Spirit. When this happens, we live in the past or the future. When we are present, however, we begin to break the top-down patterns of brain activation that keep us on autopilot. We begin to rewire these circuits in a way that frees us up to receive new information, to be surprised by new perceptions that were ruled out by our previous top-down patterns. We can fully be with others, which allows us to love them more deeply.

Perhaps this allows us to gain a greater glimpse of God. Much of our experience of God is colored by our attachment filters, which hinders our experience of the loving presence of God. The most profound tipping points occur when we see God more for who he really is. But God doesn't force us to be with him in a way that restructures our implicit knowledge of him. Instead, God invites us to be present in the moment and share in the very same love that flows between the Father, Son, and Holy Spirit, thereby receiving love into the core of our being.

When we encounter God through Scripture and contemplative practices such as prayer, it helps us to interpret our experiences and feel God's truth, which lead to an integrated knowledge of God. To know God, to be in his presence, and to participate in the love of the Trinity, is to be transformed at the very core of our being. As we cultivate this deep growth through the age-old practices of engaging with Scripture and contemplative prayer, we become more like Christ in our love for God and others. In this love we find meaning in something good that is larger than ourselves, which we'll talk about in chapter fourteen. First, we'll turn to the special role that suffering plays in deep growth.

13

Suffering Well

IN 2013, MY WIFE, LIZ, was diagnosed with breast cancer. This began a new journey for both of us—a journey of suffering and growth. Liz went through a year of treatment including multiple surgeries. For me, this journey involved the emotional pain of seeing someone I love experience fear, anxiety, uncertainty, grief, and aloneness. In addition, I went through my own feelings of sadness, fear of losing my wife, fear of my sons losing their mother, and the stress of trying to be strong for my wife and kids. Since we work at the same organization, people at work would understandably ask how Liz was doing. I would fill them in, and then retreat to my office and break down crying. I then had to pull myself together to teach a class or see a client. It was difficult to bring these issues up to the surface while holding it together to stay in work mode. Suffering entered my life in a new way, but it also led to growth in ways that wouldn't have happened without the suffering.

Suffering isn't necessary for growth, but with certain kinds of processes it can lead to growth. Why does this happen? Suffering has a way of loosening our grip on unhealthy implicit beliefs, creating the potential to shift these beliefs and depend more on God. The first step in dealing with suffering, however, is to come to grips with a myth.

Suffering isn't something we wish on ourselves or others, but our pursuit of comfort often leads us to believe the myth that the most important priority in life is to purge all suffering from our lives. This raises a key question we have to face when it comes to suffering: how, then, should we approach suffering in our lives?

My suggestion is this: we seek to suffer well and to grow closer to Christ through our suffering. This is the picture painted for us in Scripture, and it's fleshed out by psychological research. In this chapter, we'll take a look at what Scripture has to say about suffering—that we are to entrust our suffering to God, which transforms our relational knowledge and attachment filters. Then we'll look at the markers of growth through suffering that reflect shifts in our implicit relational knowledge and some practical suggestions on suffering well. We'll conclude with reflections on identifying with Christ through our suffering.[1]

BRINGING OUR SUFFERING TO GOD

Romans 8:18-28 is a key passage for understanding the suffering of the believer, culminating in the promise that "God causes everything to work together for the good of those who love God" (v. 28). This passage introduces the present sufferings of the believer (v. 18), and then describes our groanings as we wait for the end of our sufferings and the "new bodies he has promised us" (v. 23). In this groaning we receive assistance: "The Holy Spirit helps us in our weakness.... We don't know what God wants us to pray for. But the Holy Spirit prays for us with groanings that cannot be expressed in words.... in harmony with God's own will" (vv. 26-27).

The Spirit assists us in bringing our suffering to the Father. In addition to this, the Spirit comforts us in our suffering by strengthening our Father-child relationship with God, which brings us into deeper participation in Christ's Sonship with the Father. In other words, the Spirit guides us to experience and share in the love between Jesus and the Father in order to help us cope with, and even grow through, our sufferings in this life:

Now we call him, "Abba, Father." For his Spirit joins with our spirit to affirm that we are God's children. And since we are his children, we are his heirs. In fact, together with Christ we are heirs of God's glory. But if we are to share his glory, we must also share his suffering. (Romans 8:15-17)

This passage in Romans 8 is particularly striking when viewed through an attachment lens. Paul uses the vivid imagery of the groanings of childbirth to describe the suffering, a picture of visceral, gut-wrenching pain made more difficult because it's nonverbal ("groanings that cannot be expressed in words"). In an unimaginably intimate way, the Spirit attunes with our soul, taking on our groanings and bringing them to the Father. We also see the secure attachment imagery in our experience of the Father. In our distress, we cry out to the Father in the most intimate and informal way possible, "Abba!" or "Daddy!" with the knowledge, reinforced by the Spirit, that God cares and responds. The possibilities for deep change to our attachment filters are striking. In bringing our suffering to God, God helps us to know—directly through our experience of relationship with him— that we are his child whom he loves and cherishes.

Our relationships (with God and others) play a critical role in growing through suffering. We need others to help us in the process of meaning-making. We need a balance of support and positive challenge in order for growth to occur. On the one hand, without sufficient support, we feel overwhelmed, making it difficult to digest painful experiences. On the other hand, without enough challenge, we may settle for unhealthy ways of coping.

We also need to bring our suffering to God. Hardships in our lives can cause us to distance ourselves from God. Christ's example encourages us instead to struggle *in* God's loving presence. Peter notes a specific way in which Jesus turned to the Father in his suffering: he "entrusted himself" to God (I Peter 2:23 NIV). The verb tense used can be translated "*kept entrusting*" and indicates that this was a deliberate choice on Jesus' part.[2] In other words, Jesus kept handing over his sufferings to God.

Scripture gives us abundant guidance in the process of handing over our suffering to God, in the form of lament. The biblical practice of lament can be considered a kind of framework for meaning-making[3] and for integrating the two ways of knowing. Although lament occurs throughout Scripture, it's found in its purest form in the Psalms, almost 40 percent of which are psalms of lament. Lament is not merely pouring out our heart to God, nor is it merely complaining or venting. Instead, lament has a specific structure. It's a stylized form of speech consisting of common elements that define a specific trajectory. These elements include: (1) an address to God; (2) a pouring out of our suffering to God; (3) a request to God to alleviate the suffering; (4) and last but not least, an expression of trust in God.[4] This trajectory involves a transformative psychological shift from distress to praise. In praying through the lament, the experience brought about by its structure begins to restore some sense of order in the midst of chaos and pain. The shape of lament causes our verbalized experience to be molded by encountering the reality of God and his character in a powerful integration of the two ways of knowing. When we express our experience in the form of lament, we allow our experience to be interpreted by the words of the lament, and we feel the idea of God's trustworthiness. The two ways of knowing come together in an integrated knowledge that transforms our soul.

THE MARKERS OF GROWTH THROUGH SUFFERING

Not everyone grows through suffering, and suffering itself isn't the cause of growth. Growth is the result of certain processes a person goes through with respect to suffering. While growth through suffering isn't inevitable, it is possible, and we're learning in the related fields of stress-related and posttraumatic growth more from the people who experience it. Jerry, for example, is a paraplegic man who experienced profound growth following a car accident that left him paralyzed. Here's how he describes it:

This was the one thing that happened in my life that I needed to have happen; it was probably the best thing that ever happened to me. On the outside looking in that's pretty hard to swallow, I'm sure, but hey, that's the way I view it. If I hadn't experienced this and lived through it, I likely wouldn't be here today because my lifestyle previously—I was on a real self-destructive path. If I had it to do all over again, I would want it to happen the same way.[5]

When people who have grown through suffering describe the changes, several themes emerge in three broad categories: changes in philosophy of life, changes within the self, and changes in relationships.[6] People often describe these changes as "wisdom" because they reflect a deep transformation in the implicit self that rewires and reorients a person's way of being and relating to others. Within these three broad categories, there are eight markers of growth through suffering. We'll explore each of these with some examples from my own journey through my wife's cancer.

CHANGES IN PHILOSOPHY OF LIFE

In the category of philosophy of life, people who grow through suffering often report a deeper appreciation of life, a shift in their priorities, and a renewed sense of spiritual vitality. All of these changes reflect implicit beliefs or knowledge rather than strictly head knowledge.

1. A deeper appreciation for life. This growth marker includes a deeper appreciation for the simple moments in everyday life and for relationships that are often taken for granted.

One morning, between cancer treatments, my wife told me she was "grateful for the sweet ordinariness of everyday life." Going through the experience of my wife having cancer has certainly given me a much deeper appreciation for life and for living in the present. It's given me a desire to cherish my wife and children every moment I can. I don't know if my wife's life will end up shorter than we both hope for, but I do know our lives are now richer for the experience of facing cancer together.

2. Positive change in priorities. This marker includes a renewed sense that time and relationships are precious. In addition, there is often a shift toward owning one's values and priorities.

My priorities in every aspect of life were immediately impacted by my wife's cancer. Suddenly, it became clear that so many things in my life are really not that important. Mostly, these have to do with the achievements I strive after to bolster my ego. I see with more clarity that the most important thing in life is the impact I have on other people. It's the love I give and receive in relating to people every day, especially to those in my small corner of the universe—the people to whom I am particularly responsible. Time is not under my control, and I don't want to waste it on trivial things. In the work domain, I have a renewed sense of urgency to focus with laser precision on things that matter and on the areas where I can have the biggest positive impact. I experience this clarity as a gift. I don't know how or if I could have attained it without going through this experience.

3. Renewed and strengthened spiritual vitality. For many people, suffering initiates a spiritual search for significance. For some people this search ends in a decline in spiritual vitality. For many, however, the process of making sense of the suffering causes an initial decline in spirituality but eventually leads to a stronger spirituality. A stronger sense of spirituality can: (1) help people gain a sense of control over circumstances that feel uncontrollable; (2) provide comfort; (3) facilitate a stronger intimacy with God; and (4) help people find meaning in and through their suffering.

Regardless of where we are in our spirituality or relationship with God, it's important to make sense of our suffering—to find meaning and purpose in it in the context of the ultimate questions of life. For me personally, processing through my wife's cancer led to a deeper trust in God. This hasn't been a smooth process by any means, but it has strengthened my faith in God.

As I mentioned, these changes in philosophy of life go deeper than explicit knowledge, although reflection can certainly bring about a greater conceptual understanding of spiritual growth. In terms of my priorities, my explicit understanding of what my priorities should be didn't change all that much. But the experience of suffering changed how I "see" my priorities—the way I hold them and the way I know or experience them in my relationships. What was fundamentally reoriented was my gut-level, implicit knowledge of how to relate to God and others.

CHANGES WITHIN THE SELF

On the theme of changes within the self, we find that people often report increased personal strength, deeper appreciation of their vulnerability, and more acceptance of their limitations. It's noteworthy that these changes in one's sense of self often reflect a positive change in their attachment filters.

4. Increased personal strength. People often find that as they come through trials and suffering, they discover personal strength they didn't know they had. They tend to see themselves as stronger, wiser, and more resilient after going through a significant trial.[7] Being pushed to the limit and coming out on the other side has a way of doing that.

I never knew how I would respond to something like my wife going through cancer. Would I freak out? Disengage from my family? Sadly, many men leave their wives after breast cancer. Well, now I know. This is not to say that my response has been perfect by any stretch, but I know that my love for my wife has grown stronger, and that I can weather more storms of life than I thought.

5. Deeper appreciation of vulnerability. People who grow through suffering also tend to report a greater acceptance of their vulnerabilities and limitations.[8] Suffering challenges our assumptions of control, allowing for the possibility that in our helplessness we can learn to be more dependent on God's Spirit and more connected to the love shared among the Trinity. It's noteworthy that an acute sense of helplessness is linked with the greatest growth in the posttraumatic stress literature. Only in this state do we fully recognize ourselves as creatures before a powerful God—but a God who is also merciful and loving. Character changes are reported frequently as well.[9]

Through my wife's cancer experience, I came to realize that the reality of uncertainty is deeper than the illusion of certainty I used to live in. This realization brings a strange sense of peace. This experience has confronted me with my fundamental vulnerability and need for others. While not easy, I'm more at peace with it now.

6. Acceptance of limitations. Many people who grow through suffering report an increased sense of peace and acceptance with their limitations.

Through my own journey, I have come to grips more with the fact that I can't control my emotions or my circumstances. I've known this in my head, and to some extent in my gut, but now it is more deeply ingrained in my soul. I am a limited human being; I can't make cancer go away. I can't fix all the problems that come my way. Less energy is taken up fighting against my limitations. Being more aware of them helps me to empathize with and have compassion for others.

Knowing a new level of personal strength, finding a sense of peace with vulnerability, and accepting our limitations also reflect changes in the implicit self. Feeling a sense of peace with our limitations is not explicit knowledge; it's implicit relational knowledge. It's a knowing in the soul that permeates our way of being.

CHANGES IN RELATIONSHIPS

With respect to relationships, suffering often brings about an overall stronger sense of closeness to and appreciation of others. More specifically, people tend to report increased emotional expressiveness and self-disclosure, and a greater sense of compassion for the suffering of others.[10] One study found that while all forms of prayer were positively correlated with growth in suffering, contemplative forms of prayer had the strongest relationship.[11] This type of prayer may facilitate a meaning-making process in God's presence, which is necessary for growth.

7. Increased emotional expressiveness and self-disclosure. In the wake of suffering, many people find themselves expressing their emotions in a more open way. This often strengthens relationships and social support as one becomes more willing to accept help. People experiencing suffering need to talk about their experiences. Their deeper appreciation of vulnerability in conjunction with this often leads to more self-disclosure, which also improves relationships.

This one has been difficult for me. One of my roles is that of therapist, so my training and personality are oriented toward listening and not necessarily self-disclosing. I think this is partly an occupational hazard. However, as I've talked about my experiences with close friends, it has strengthened my relationships and made me more comfortable with my vulnerability.

8. Compassion, empathy, and intentionality. Many people report a deeper sense compassion for people as a result of experiencing suffering. It's also common for people to put more effort into relationships because of newfound clarity about how important they are.

The whole experience of my wife's cancer has made me acutely sensitive and empathic toward others who are suffering. Recently, a friend called and told me about a serious illness his wife was experiencing. I was immediately cut to the heart and moved with compassion. I wanted to do something, anything, to help, because I know something of this pain. There were times when it would have been difficult for me to respond with compassion because I was lost in my own pain. This growth, again, doesn't happen automatically. You have to process your own pain enough to be able to focus on others in order to respond with compassion. There are probably many other forms of wisdom that people gain from processing suffering, but these are a few common ones, and ones I've experienced in my journey.

As with shifts in the self, changes in relationships that can result from suffering reflect deep, relational knowledge. Our attachment filters get rewired so we connect more deeply with others. As we come to terms with our own story, we are able to come to know others' stories with a greater sense of compassion.

SUFFERING WELL

Some people who go through a trial spiral downward, never to return to their previous level of functioning, whereas others not only rebound but end up more gracious, virtuous, and wise for the experience. These are the people we want to be around and from whom we want to learn. It's easy in our culture to implicitly buy into the myth that our highest priority should be to purge suffering from our lives. As we saw in Scripture, however, we are called to bring our suffering to God and to allow God to grow us through it. It turns out that it is possible to grow through suffering, but we have to engage in specific processes that facilitate growth.

In this section, drawing on a growing research literature and my own experience, I want to focus on how to grow relationally through suffering. What does it look like to suffer well? I'll highlight here five practices that are backed by research that help us grow through times of struggle.

1. Find safe relationships to process suffering. Suffering is meant to be faced in relationship. We all need people to walk alongside us on the journey of suffering. We know from research and our experience that social support plays a huge role in helping people cope with trials and eventually grow from them. You need people who are safe for you to express your true feelings about your pain. Close connections are a positive outcome for those who grow through suffering, but they are also a mechanism for it. This means you need put effort into reaching out to people who can be with you in the midst of a painful time.

This was crucial for both my wife and I during her cancer treatment and even now after the treatment. She talked with numerous friends regularly about her experiences. She also reached out to several women who had been through a similar diagnosis, and this was very helpful. Likewise, I have several friends who checked in with me regularly and listened. The key to growing through suffering is to not feel alone in it. You may not be able to change the circumstances, but others will help you not feel alone in the midst of suffering. Even though it's difficult when you're going through a hard time, you need to do your part in reaching out and being vulnerable (and a deeper appreciation of vulnerability is one of the positive changes people tend to experience when they grow through suffering).

2. Approach and express emotions. Once you find people to walk with you on this journey, you need to approach and express your emotions, rather than suppress and run from them. Research shows that approaching and expressing your emotions related to suffering leads to positive outcomes. Conversely, research indicates that suppressing emotion leads to negative outcomes, like increased rates of anxiety and depression. You need emotionally safe relationships in order to trust that your vulnerable emotions will be handled with care and compassion. When you express your true emotions in the context of safe relationships, it sets in motion a series of positive processes. You connect more deeply to others, which is healing in itself. In addition, you begin to discover the meaning of your suffering in the context of your life story.

This was definitely true in my relationship with my wife and in our relationships with others. There were times we wanted to be strong for each other and not express painful, vulnerable feelings; there is a place for that. But when we did express these things, we grew closer to each other and gained a greater understanding of ourselves. One morning, after treatment had been over for several months, my wife and I were talking on a walk when she broke down crying and told me that she didn't want to die, and that not a day goes by that she doesn't fear the cancer coming back. That was hard for her to share and painful for me to hear. But it drew us closer together and gave us both a deeper understanding of where we were in the ongoing journey.

3. Process the emotions of suffering all the way through. Once you start talking about and feeling the pain of your suffering, stay with the feelings until you get to the end of the emotional arc. This principle comes from what is sometimes called a "functional" theory of emotion, which suggests that emotions are fundamentally adaptive. As we talked about earlier, emotions are automatic evaluations of the events in life. They provide crucial information and orient you to what is important for your well-being. For example, sadness is adaptive because it helps you grieve a loss.

Emotions have a natural arc or progression in terms of their intensity and clarity. As you begin to feel the impact of your trial, you may start off ruminating about the situation. It's important not to stop at this phase. You need to experience your emotions more fully to obtain the adaptive benefits.

As you engage in this process with people you trust, and continue the arc of the feeling, the meaning becomes clearer and it helps you to feel and to discover yourself and the meaning of your suffering to you. There is a sense of relief as you experience the full measure of your own emotional truth—the core of your emotion; this is you. You are moving from unintentional rumination to meaning-making. And when you experience this, you feel more connected to others and less alone in your suffering. As my wife and I processed all the emotions related to the cancer, sadness and anxiety gradually transformed into an acceptance of the reality of our new journey, and at times glimmers of gratitude for the wisdom we're gaining.

4. Reflect on and reorder your priorities. Trials have a way of making you re-think your priorities in life. This can help you grow, but you have to actively reflect on what is truly important in life and then be intentional about changing routines and habits in ways that align with your revised priorities.

For me, this showed up in three ways. First, it means spending more time with my wife and kids and cherishing the present moment with them. It means deciding to be fully present with them when we're together. Whether you realize it or not, you are deciding to either be fully present with people or to not be fully present with them. Second, this in turn means working less and accepting my limitations. And maybe on a good day, even embracing my limitations. It means leaving the next item on my to-do list when the time has come to do something else, and to trust that I will get the most important work done. Third, it means finding my identity more in my relationships than in my accomplishments. Accomplishments are good, but only insofar as they serve the purpose of promoting good in the lives of others.

5. Use your experiences of suffering to help others. Many people find an immense sense of meaning in helping others who've gone through similar trials. Even if others didn't go through the exact same trial, using your pain to express empathy and compassion for others is a way of redeeming your suffering. It's a way of creating meaning out of it.

Others did this for my wife, and she is now doing this for others. My wife recently had a long conversation with a friend whose sister was just diagnosed with cancer. This helped her friend and it helped my wife to bring something good out of her pain.

This may take some time before you are ready, so don't rush yourself. But when you're ready you'll know it. You'll notice others' suffering more quickly and feel with others more deeply because of what you've been through. Then put these feelings into action and express compassion for others.

When we encounter suffering, we all have a choice. We can pursue comfort at all costs, or we can decide, in our heart of hearts, to step onto the pathway toward growth in character. As we take this step, we are encouraged to bring our suffering to God. When we do this, the Spirit helps us create an intimate connection with the Father who has deep compassion for us. The imagery here is that of a young child running into the outstretched arms of Daddy. This is an active process of *entrusting* our sufferings to God. Scripture provides guidance on how to engage in this process in the form of lament. Lament, in which we pour out our suffering to God, ask God to relieve our suffering, and declare our trust in God, is an act of faith that also builds our faith in the process. It helps to transform our implicit knowledge of God from anger and disappointment to deeper dependence and trust.

Psychological research also provides helpful guidelines for how to grow through suffering. This research suggests the importance of processing your emotions and priorities in safe relationships, and using your suffering to help others. As you pursue the path of suffering well, you will find opportunities to identify with Christ. As you entrust your suffering to God, you emulate Christ, become more like him, and experience a certain type of intimacy with Christ that can only come from relational knowledge of Christ's pattern of suffering—suffering in complete surrender to the Father in an act of profound love for others. This is the ultimate goal of suffering well. We turn now to the final topic on transformation, and the broader context for deep growth: belonging in spiritual community.

14

Born *to* Belong

WHEN I WAS IN THE ARMY, my wife and I were uprooted from our long-standing community in Los Angeles, where we attended graduate school and where I grew up. The Army provided some measure of companionship, but it didn't meet a deeper need for Christian community.

THE NEED FOR BELONGING

We all have a fundamental human need to belong to a community. We need "our people" who understand us, support us, encourage us, and challenge us to grow. Secular communities fulfill some of these needs. Yet secular communities leave a gap in our sense of meaning and purpose as Christians; we know and feel that we're called to a community that has a deeper purpose and a higher good. The new family of God is rooted in the love of the Trinity and is the paradigmatic expression of community—the ultimate group to which we desire to belong. As children of God, we know we belong to the body of Christ. But we also need to *feel* like we belong to God's new family—to be part of the ultimate family that is centered around God's love.

Yet this experience of belonging too often eludes us as we feel disappointment in our church communities, which to some extent reflects the connection crisis in our larger society. This was part of our story during our major moves while I was in the Army. Liz and I attended a church in Washington, DC, where I was first stationed. It was a good church, but as outsiders who were new to the area, it was difficult to break in and feel truly connected to the body of Christ there. Knowing we would likely be moving a year later made it all the more difficult. After the next move, we again settled on a new church and attended regularly. We built a few relationships there and tried to get involved in ministry. For a variety of reasons, it felt like a struggle to gain traction in serving and becoming more deeply connected with the congregation. Looking back, I think there were many factors, including my own unrealistic expectations as a young adult and some particular areas of dysfunction within that church. Regardless of the causes, we were left feeling disconnected and longing for a deeper sense of community.

Struggles in finding strong spiritual community are not uncommon. While such experiences undoubtedly occur across all age groups, research in my lab, led by Chelsea Kreuger, found that these experiences are particularly common among young adults in their late twenties (late emerging adults) as they are trying to settle into adulthood.[1] Through in-depth interviews, we discovered that late emerging adults often felt lonely, hurt, and a lack of sense of belonging in their spiritual communities. They also reported frequent unmet expectations that included feeling not accepted or known in their church community. This all contributed to an overall sense of disappointment in their spiritual communities.

For example, Hannah and her husband left a church after feeling that no one engaged in authentic relationship with them:

We haven't really felt supported or accepted or that we belong in the community of the church. . . . But after about a year of being on the launch team and then eventually we launch the church, we still didn't have any, even good friends or people that knew the details of my health problems. So, I think, it's like another year, we were trying to make the decision to stay at the church or leave, and we ended up leaving and kind of felt like no one noticed.

In another example, Sophia described unmet expectations with respect to a ministry in which she was involved:

The ministry that we started at the church, we had really high hopes for. And it became evident that our leader, the pastor, just is more of a macro picture leader and didn't give us the proper orientation or authority, or division of labor. It just didn't go well, so to speak.

Brandon, likewise, shared that many of his struggles or disappointments have been experienced within the church:

Yeah, in fact the church . . . that has been where most of my trials and struggles come from. It's been in church. It hasn't been outside of church. Outside of the church, people are receiving people, you know, accepting people and understanding. It is inside of the church that you deal with, you know, the contradiction and the most hurt, you know.

When we encounter such struggles, it's natural to become disillusioned with our spiritual community. At times, we may feel overlooked, not included, or not valued. We may feel the community isn't meeting our needs, doesn't reflect our values, or has too much conflict. I have worked with many clients who felt this way at times, and I've struggled with this myself as I noted above. Communities in the early New Testament church also struggled with conflict and tension among their various members. When we become disillusioned, the temptation we face is to *disengage* in various ways: (1) we search for a "better" church community; (2) we stay on the edges of community; or (3) we convince ourselves that we're better off practicing "solo Christianity." These temptations are almost automatic due to the individualistic and consumeristic culture in the Western world. When we disengage from Christian community, it becomes fragmented, and we collectively fail to create a new social order of love and to shine God's light to the world.

This raises a crucial question: how do we go about building a sense of belonging in our spiritual communities, especially in the face of the conflict and disappointments that will inevitably occur? The answer is, in a word: *together*. We build spiritual community—a place of belonging—as we travel together along the journey with one another. Moreover, this side of heaven, we will always be transforming our church communities so they increasingly reflect God and provide a contrast-society that shines God's light to the world. Next, we'll briefly explore several components of belonging, while highlighting a few principles to help shape our mindset and guide our actions toward building a sense of belonging to God's new family.

THE STRUCTURE OF BELONGING:
SHARED IDENTITY, EXPERIENCE, AND PURPOSE

As we build God's new family, we must facilitate the experience of three interrelated aspects that comprise the structure of belonging: a shared identity, a shared experience, and a shared purpose. 1 Peter 2:9-10 provides a brief but helpful picture of these aspects of belonging in the body of Christ.

First, we share an *identity* as God's "chosen people" and as "royal priests, a holy nation, God's very own possession" (v. 9). God's chosen people are described as a new family. Jesus promised those who left their families to follow him that God would be their Father (Matthew 23:9) and that they would have many mothers, brothers, and sisters (Mark 10:29-30). In this way, Jesus established the church as a new family, consisting of all who follow Jesus. This way of thinking about the church is the first and most foundational of the metaphors used by Paul. We might even say that it transcends a mere metaphor, describing a new reality. "Brothers" and "sisters" became the most common way of referring to and thinking about one another in the context of the church. This identity as siblings was rooted in the common experience of being sons and daughters of God.

We find our deepest identity or sense of who we are in being a child of God and sibling to our brothers and sisters in Christ. We share this identity with each other and so it's a significant aspect of what bonds us to the new family of God. We belong to the body of Christ because we are all children of God. In our gatherings, we need to practice reminding ourselves of our common identity to promote a sense of belonging that will in turn build commitment and mutual love.

Second, we all share the *experience* of having received God's mercy (1 Peter 2:10). While everyone's salvation story differs, we share the basic experience of receiving God's forgiveness and being adopted as children of God. This is a very formative experience that rewires our implicit relational knowledge and bonds us together. It's also an experience that we encounter over and over again throughout our lives. In addition, we share the experience of corporate worship as we sing, pray, receive Communion together, and hear and respond to God's Word. As we gather in small and large groups, we need to rekindle and remind ourselves of our shared experience. One powerful way of doing this is sharing our testimonies and other ways we have experienced God's mercy. In my Sunday school class, we have times devoted to sharing how God is working in our lives. In our worship services, we also periodically set aside time for people to share their testimonies and the ongoing work of God in their lives. It's always uplifting and these times renew our shared experience of God's mercy and grace, as well as our shared identity as children of God. We belong precisely because we share a profound, life-changing experience.

Finally, we share a common *purpose* to "show others the goodness of God" (1 Peter 2:9). The new family of God is supposed to collectively demonstrate God's love and be a visible sign of salvation for all nations. God's plan is that his people would draw the nations to himself by being a contrast-society living out a new social order of love.[2] This new family of God is to be a radiant city on the hill (Matthew 5:13-16). Our common purpose, then, is to develop this new social order of love, which contrasts with the values of secular society, and thereby reflect God to the world. This is something we can only fully do collectively.

When we gather as a local expression of the family of God, we need to intentionally remind ourselves of our common purpose. We don't belong solely in order to socialize with people like us and stay in our comfort zone. This would amount to a thin sense of belonging. Rather, we experience belonging to the family of God in part because we're working on a mission together—the ultimate mission. We are working with God and each other to bring about the kingdom of heaven. Each local community plays its own role, but within our local spiritual community we work side by side with each other to create a community characterized by the mutual love of the Trinity and to offer this mutual love and belonging to the world. We belong because we share the most important purpose of all.

The Glue of Belonging: Commitment and Mutuality

A healthy spiritual community is the responsibility of all of its members, who must all work in cooperation with the Holy Spirit. Each of us is creating the very community to which we desire to belong and from which we desire to receive support. This means we're all accountable for doing our part in building spiritual communities that: (1) we desire to belong to; (2) exhibit a new social order of love; and (3) display God's love to the world.

When we become disillusioned, our temptation is to focus on what we're getting or not getting from our community. This is understandable. We all feel this way at times, and we all need support and love from others in our community when we get stuck in such an emotional place. We may need to reach out and let others know how we are feeling. Making ourselves vulnerable requires great courage and is the fuel that drives authentic connection and transformation in community.

Although we need this help from other members of the body, because we're all interdependent, we also need to do our part in refocusing our mindset, in concert with the Holy Spirit, on how we can help create the community that truly shines God's light. This requires a deep commitment to the community. In order to be part of building something larger than ourselves, we have to stay and remain engaged when things get difficult. As I noted, this goes very much against the grain of our individualistic society. It's much easier to leave when things become challenging and painful, and this is almost normal in our culture. When we leave at the first sign of difficulties, however, we are more likely to repeat old, unhealthy relational patterns. Deep change, in contrast, happens through long-term relationships that allow us to face our pain and to become more securely attached. This is consistent with the family bonds that comprise our church communities.

The family of God is a new reality that both shines God's light to the world and foreshadows the fullness of heaven. This is not to say that there are never times to leave a local church community, but it is to say that allegiance to family in our spiritual community should be paramount in our decision-making. As we consider our commitments to spiritual community, we would do well to remember that we're building something that foreshadows heaven, and that will someday come to full expression in heaven.

With our commitment in place, part of our contribution is to be on the lookout for our brothers and sisters in Christ who may be feeling disillusioned, frustrated, or may just be hurting. Just as we receive support during times like these, we bring this love full circle by offering it to others in our community. As we are reminded of our shared identity, experience, and purpose, we find ourselves moved to love our brothers and sisters in Christ. We desire their well-being and we seek connection. As we noted earlier, this means we strive to understand what the other needs in order to promote their well-being.

As in any relationship, spiritual community requires mutuality, but at the collective level. This doesn't happen in a linear manner. Each person gives and receives to different people and subgroups, but at the collective level everyone and the community grows. We must commit ourselves to the higher good of family members and to the community as a whole. When we do this, mutual love becomes a reality—a love that reflects the Trinity and shows the world who God is.

I've had the privilege of being a member of a Sunday school class for over eighteen years that embodies this commitment and mutual love. People tend to remain in the group for a long time. Many of the families have been a part of the group for over a decade and we've experienced all facets of life together, including triumphs and tragedies. Most of the members of the group are committed to the group as a whole and volunteer their time and talents for the good of the group. While our community is certainly not perfect, and occasional frustrations and tensions arise, there is a distinct sense of mutual love in our class. People reach out and offer emotional and practical support to others. The central point is that, on balance, everyone takes responsibility for the community and invests in the good of the group. Because of this, we all receive even while we all give to the group, stimulating a mutual love that reflects the Trinity.

THE BALANCE IN BELONGING: AUTHORITATIVE
SPIRITUAL COMMUNITIES

Communities grow and help their members grow by being authoritative. But what does it mean for a community to be *authoritative*? And what does this look like in practice?

To provide some background on this aspect of community, we look to the work of a group of scholars and practitioners who treat children and do research on child development.[3] This group was commissioned to address the deteriorating mental and behavioral health of US children, and to propose policy solutions to the problems. The Commission on Children at Risk concluded that the crisis stems from a lack of connectedness: close connections to other people and deep connections to moral and spiritual meaning.

After extensive research, they attributed the decline in children's mental health to the weakening of "authoritative communities" in the

United States, and advocated for the strengthening of these kinds of communities. Drawing on the concept of authoritative parenting, they defined authoritative communities as "groups of people who are committed to one another over time and who model and pass on at least part of what it means to be a good person and live a good life."[4] In other words, authoritative communities are communities that blend warmth and structure.

An authoritative community includes, among others, the following six characteristics: (1) it treats others as ends in themselves, rather than as means to an end; (2) it is warm and nurturing; (3) it establishes clear limits and expectations; (4) it is multigenerational; (5) it reflects and transmits a shared understanding of what it means to be a good person; and (6) it is philosophically oriented to the equal dignity of all persons and to the principle of love of neighbor.[5] Like authoritative parenting, authoritative communities balance and integrate warmth and empathy on the one hand, and moral structure on the other hand. They are neither permissive, with an "anything goes" attitude, nor authoritarian, with a cold, rigid focus on rules. In contrast, these communities are supportive while at the very same time expecting certain behaviors, values, and character traits because they are good for the individual's well-being and for the community as a whole. Authoritative communities help members to become a certain kind of person through intergenerational connection, warmth, and moral boundaries.

Authoritative communities include a wide array of civic, educational, community service, recreational, cultural, and religious groups that serve and/or include children.[6] James Comer of Yale University has done work showing that when schools begin to function as authoritative communities, they improve children's education and overall lives. Another prime example of an authoritative community that is widely known is the YMCA, which helped sponsor the *Hardwired to Connect* report written by the Commission on Children at Risk.

It's not difficult to see the similarities between "authoritative communities" and the type of spiritual community that comprises the body of Christ. In fact, much of the research supporting the value of authoritative communities comes from research on church participation. Hundreds of studies have supplied evidence that church participation exerts a protective influence on factors including mortality, hypertension, suicide, promiscuous sexual behaviors, drug and alcohol use, and delinquency.[7] In addition, participation in organized religion increases well-being, hope, purpose, meaning in life, self-esteem, and educational attainment. These findings support the premise that communities that establish moral expectations in a warm, supportive climate tend to decrease participation in problematic behaviors and increase prosocial behaviors leading to positive outcomes.

Why is it that these kinds of communities are able to exercise a powerful moral influence on their members? Part of the answer comes from what psychiatrist Barbara Stilwell has called "the moralization of attachment."[8] Stilwell describes a process through which infant-parent attachment interacts to form a security-empathy-oughtness representation within the child's mind. In other words, implicit feelings of security or insecurity are paired with the (often nonverbal and unconscious) messages from parents about which behaviors are pleasing or non-pleasing, prohibited or encouraged, worthy of attention or not worthy of attention. In this way there is a biological readiness to moralize behavior based on seeking parental connection. When people of various ages form part of a close-knit spiritual community, their internalization of the values of the community goes hand-in-hand with emotional connections with members of that community.

The local church, when it's functioning well, clearly fits the description of an authoritative community. When I was in high school, I had the good fortune to become a member of a church that functioned as an authoritative community. I was involved in a small youth group that fostered close relationships with my peers and several youth pastors. The youth pastors were encouraging, warm, and supportive, but I also internalized a set of values that I heard them teach and saw them live out. It was clear that there was a model of "the good life" we were striving for and moral boundaries that supported such a life. Certain behaviors were out of bounds because they didn't promote the good life—they didn't honor God or our brothers and sisters in Christ. I knew this based on the way my youth pastors and the senior pastor treated others with kindness, and also the way they lovingly confronted problematic behaviors in members of our community.

For example, on one occasion one of my youth pastors and his wife got into an argument, which led to him canceling an event. He could have covered this up, but instead, afterwards he shared with me how he felt he had hurt his wife and that he apologized and asked for forgiveness. They both shared openly, but appropriately, about their relationship and this event, and it led to meaningful discussions about the importance of humility and forgiveness. Perhaps more important than the discussions, as critical as they were, I saw warmth and moral structure modeled in their relationship. Hurtful interpersonal behavior wasn't condoned, and yet forgiveness was freely offered, and warmth was quickly restored. Because I developed close relationships with my pastors and many adults (valuable intergenerational connections), I wanted to please them and be accepted by them, which in turn caused me to take on their values as my own. This is the moralization of attachment in action.

In New Testament teachings on the church, there is a strong emphasis on the importance of "speaking the truth in love." As we do this, Paul tells us in Ephesians, "we will grow to become in every respect the mature body of him who is the head, that is, Christ. From him the whole body, joined and held together by every supporting ligament, grows and builds itself up in love, as each part does its work" (Ephesians 4:15-16 NIV). From a social science perspective, the research on authoritative communities concludes with the same bottom line: we need relationships, but we need specific kinds of relationships that will authoritatively provide us with a true story within which we can find our own story and identity.

THE UNIT OF BELONGING: SMALL GROUPS

When my wife and I moved to Washington, DC, we joined a large church. It was wonderful in many ways and had a lot of resources, but we felt lost within the large congregation. Even the young adult group was quite large, which presented some challenges in feeling connected. We've all probably had the experience of joining a community and feeling lost in a large group. While larger groups have certain benefits, we also need smaller groups to help us grow. In our spiritual communities, it's important to attend to the size of our various groups.

The first two tiers of small groups—up to six members or fifteen members, respectively—are where attachment and closer relationships can develop, which have the potential to promote transformational change. In his work on building community, Peter Block echoes the importance of the small group, suggesting it is "the unit of transformation."[9] We might extend this idea to suggest that small groups are the unit of belonging. In referring to small groups, I don't necessarily mean a small group program. Rather, I am thinking of any small group that meets regularly within the larger context of the body of Christ.

Larger groups within our spiritual communities are important, but we must strive to connect people in first and second tier small groups, because these groups create the conditions for intimacy, authentic relatedness, a unique valuing of each person, and meaningful dialogue. As members of the community, we can each focus on creating the experience of belonging as we gather. This requires being present in the moment and recognizing that we are now inhabiting a sense of belonging to God's family. Within a smaller group, it is possible to foster intimacy, authenticity, and a more personal sense of belonging.

For example, in my Sunday school class, we structure time for sharing meaningful things about our lives, which engenders a sense of closeness. We strive to create an environment in which it feels safe to share struggles, promoting authenticity. We attempt to model for each other humility and an ongoing process of growth—the mindset that none of us has "arrived" and each of us needs God's grace every day.

This creates an environment in which everyone is uniquely valued. There is an implicit understanding that each person is important, and this value is inhabited as the group is responsive to the needs of each person as they arise. Sharing struggles and important things about our lives, in turn, creates the safety for true dialogue.

In our small groups, we must intentionally promote meaningful dialogue, which is all too often absent in our gatherings. Real dialogue, David Benner notes, is challenging because it goes beyond the simple exchange of ideas or opinions. Dialogue, rather, is "exploration and discovery through conversational engagement."[10] It's designed to promote awareness and insight and seeks mutual understanding. Dialogue is an "I-Thou" encounter in which the purpose of the conversation is simply to meet each other. It requires an openness and surrender to the process. In dialogue we go with the process by attuning to the others' emotions, listening for their emotional truth, and sharing our emotional truth in turn. As we do this, something new is created and discovered within each person and the group.

Dialogue creates personal or relational knowledge of the self and other, which leads to an expanded and enriched capacity for love. In dialogue we experience something of the essence or core of the other person. As Benner puts it, "The 'other' becomes present, not merely in one's imagination or feelings, but in the depths of one's being."[11]

While time and structure to promote dialogue will only be one of the activities within a spiritual community, it's important that we create the space and psychological safety for this. Because dialogue involves risk and vulnerability, it requires safety, and this is best accomplished in small groups. I suggested in chapter nine that love is comprised of goodwill and connection, which further involves mutual closeness. Dialogue is a form of mutual closeness in which we reveal important things about ourselves and receive the revelations of others with care and compassion. Dialogue, then, is a form of love that creates the very fabric of our communities. Because of the power of this relational knowledge and experience, dialogue promotes a deep sense of belonging. We belong because we discover ourselves, others, and Christ anew within the small groups of our communities.

With this, we have come to the end of our journey together. We've touched on the ways that we have, collectively, become more relationally and spiritually disconnected. A sense of emptiness and loneliness is on the rise; we're searching for meaning in a fragmented world.

Thankfully, this isn't the end of the story. As image bearers, we are born to connect. Relationships are where we find the meaning that defines our lives. It is deep, intimate, loving connections, bearing the mark of our triune God, that transform and rewire our souls. The core of this transformation has to do with love, as we reflect our triune God who is love. We saw that attachment-type relationships, and the relational knowledge that undergirds them, are foundational for spiritual growth, as they shape our implicit self and capacity to love. We concluded with a call for life in community as the new family of God— the kind of spiritual community that blends warmth and moral structure, and that in itself becomes the goal as together we more fully reflect God's image. We are, indeed, loved into loving in the context of community. When we, as the body of Christ, collectively love each other, and extend this love by bringing compassion to the world, especially to those who are marginalized, we act in the name of the Trinity and reflect the image of God in which we were made. This is ultimately how we will find meaning in a fragmented world.

Acknowledgments

MANY PEOPLE have helped this book become a reality. I'd like to thank all my colleagues at Rosemead School of Psychology, past and present, for providing a safe and grace-filled community in which to grow as a scholar, therapist, and follower of Christ. Likewise, my students at Rosemead have allowed me to be part of their journey and have provided helpful feedback on portions of the book. I'd like to thank Kerilee Van Schooten and Samantha Moe for providing helpful feedback on portions of the book. I'm grateful to all my clients, past and present, who have given me the great privilege of being part of their journey of healing and growth. They have inspired me and have shaped the content of this book through what I have learned in our work together. I am so grateful to have been able to partner again with InterVarsity Press on this project. The entire team has been amazing. In particular I'd like to thank my editor, Ethan McCarthy, who believed in the message of *The Connected Life* from the beginning, and significantly improved the book with his keen editorial eye. Thanks also go to Rachel Hastings, Lori Neff, and the entire marketing team, for their diligence and expertise in getting the word out about the book. Finally, I am very grateful to my wife, Liz. Throughout the project, she provided unwavering emotional support and frequent, very helpful feedback on my writing and the content of the book.

Notes

1. The Causes of Our Connection Crisis

[1]Judith Wallerstein, Julia Lewis, and Sandra Blakeslee, *The Unexpected Legacy of Divorce* (New York: Hyperion, 2000), xxxii.

[2]Niobe Way et al., "Introduction: The Crisis of Connection," in *The Crisis of Connection: Roots, Consequences, and Solutions*, eds. Niobe Way et al., (New York: NYU Press, 2018), 1-62.

[3]Martin Seligman in Robert D. Putnam, *Bowling Alone: The Collapse and Revival of American Community* (New York: Simon & Schuster, 2000), 261.

[4]Vivek Murthy, "Work and the Loneliness Epidemic: Reducing Isolation at Work is Good for Business," *Harvard Business Review*, September 26, 2017, https://hbr.org/cover-story/2017/09/work-and-the-loneliness-epidemic.

[5]*Cigna U.S. Loneliness Index: Survey of 20,000 Americans Examining Behaviors Driving Loneliness in the United States* (Cigna: Ipsos, 2018), accessed May 26, 2018, www.multivu.com/players/English/8294451-cigna-us-loneliness-survey/.

[6]Wallerstein, Lewis, and Blakeslee, *The Unexpected Legacy of Divorce*, xxviii.

[7]Paul R. Amato, "Research on Divorce: Continuing Trends and New Developments," *Journal of Marriage and Family* 72, no. 3 (June 2010): 650-66.

[8]Andrew Cherlin, "Demographic Trends in the United States: A Review of Research in the 2000s," *Journal of Marriage and Family* 72, no. 3 (June 2010): 405.

[9]Cherlin, "Demographic Trends in the United States," 403-19. Scholars refer to the trend of children being more likely to have a parent living elsewhere as the separation of household and family, or the weakened correspondence between household and family. When children of divorced or separated parents have contact with nonresident parents, the family can be said to extend across two households.

[10]Commission on Children at Risk, *Hardwired to Connect: The New Scientific Case for Authoritative Communities* (New York: Institute for American Values, 2003).

[11]One study reported that children born to cohabitating couples are at least twice as likely to have their parents separate as those children whose parents are married at the time of their birth. See Patrick Heuveline, Jeffrey M. Timberlake, and Frank F. Furstenberg, "Shifting Childrearing to Single Mothers: Results from 17 Western Countries," *Population & Development Review* 29, no. 1 (March 2003): 47-71.

[12]Amato, "Research on Divorce," 650-66.

[13]For studies on developmental outcomes of attachment, see Klaus E. Grossmann, Karin Grossmann, and Everett Waters, eds., *Attachment from Infancy to Adulthood: The Major Longitudinal Studies* (New York: Guilford Press, 2005). For a review of attachment to God and God images, see Todd W. Hall and Annie Fujikawa, "God Images and the Sacred" in *APA Handbook of Psychology, Religion, and Spirituality*, editor in chief Kenneth I. Pargament (Washington, DC: American Psychological Association, 2013), 277-92.

[14]Peter Fonagy, H. Steele, and Miriam Steele, "Maternal Representations of Attachment During Pregnancy Predict the Organization of Infant-Mother Attachment at One Year of Age," *Child Development* 62 (1991): 891-905.

[15]Amato, "Research on Divorce," 650-66.

[16]L. Laumann-Billings and R. E. Emery, "Distress Among Young Adults from Divorced Families," *Journal of Family Psychology* 14, no. 4 (December 2000): 671-87.

[17]Elizabeth Marquardt, *Between Two Worlds: The Inner Lives of Children of Divorce* (New York: Crown Publishers, 2005).

[18]"Purpose and Ethics," The Lions Clubs (website), accessed November 10, 2017, www.lionsclubs.org/en/discover-our-clubs/purpose-and-ethics.

[19]Putnam, *Bowling Alone*, 19.

[20]Commission on Children at Risk, *Hard Wired to Connect*.

[21]Putnam, *Bowling Alone*, 107.

[22]Putnam, *Bowling Alone*, 183-84.

[23]Putnam, *Bowling Alone*, 184.

[24]Marshall McLuhan, *Understanding Media: The Extensions of Man* (New York: Signet Books, 1963).

[25]Commission on Children at Risk, *Hard Wired to Connect*.

[26]Putnam, *Bowling Alone*, 283-84.

[27]Putnam, *Bowling Alone*, 283.

[28]Putnam, *Bowling Alone*, 272.

[29]Putnam, *Bowling Alone*, 273.

[30]Putnam, *Bowling Alone*, 274-75.

2. THE SPIRITUAL EFFECTS OF OUR CONNECTION CRISIS

[1]Barna Research Group and Navigators, *The State of Discipleship: Research Conducted Among Christian Adults, Church Leaders, Exemplar Discipleship Ministries and Christian Educators* (Ventura, CA: Barna Research Group, 2015), 60.

[2]Barna, *The State of Discipleship*, 84.

[3]Barna, *The State of Discipleship*, 45.

[4]Kendra L. Bailey et al., "Spirituality at a Crossroads: A Grounded Theory of Christian Emerging Adults," *Journal of Psychology of Religion & Spirituality* 8, no. 2 (2016): 99-109 , https://doi.org/10.1037/rel10000059.

[5]Bailey et al., "Spirituality at a Crossroads," 106.

[6]Bailey et al., "Spirituality at a Crossroads," 106.

3. MISGUIDED SPIRITUALITY

[1]Portions of this chapter are adapted from Todd W. Hall, "We're Loved into Loving," invited keynote presentation for the Mind Your Heart Conference, Biola University Center for Christian Thought, January 31, 2014, https://cct.biola.edu/we-re-loved-into-loving/.

4. WE KNOW MORE THAN WE CAN SAY

[1]*Good Will Hunting*, directed by Gus Van Sant (Los Angeles: Miramax, 1998).

[2]*Good Will Hunting*, Van Sant.

[3]Christopher Bollas, *The Shadow of the Object: Psychoanalysis of the Unthought Known* (New York: Columbia University Press, 1987). This provocative phrase seems to have been coined by British psychoanalyst Christopher Bollas, who may have drawn this from a statement Freud made in commenting on the characteristic response of the patient who has become aware of something "forgotten": "As a matter of fact, I've always known it; only I've never thought of it." Quote cited in David J. Wallin, *Attachment in Psychotherapy* (New York: Guilford, 2007), 115.

[4]Malcolm Gladwell, *Blink* (New York: Little, Brown, 2005), 7.

[5]Gladwell, *Blink*, 23.

[6]Michael Polanyi, *Personal Knowledge: Towards a Post-Critical Philosophy* (Chicago: University of Chicago Press, 1958).

[7]This section is adapted with permission from "If You Want to Succeed in Life, Don't Ignore Emotions—Train Them," *Dr. Todd Hall* blog, accessed March 14, 2022, www.drtoddhall.com/if-you-want-to-succeed-in-life-dont-ignore-emotions-train-them/.

[8]Paul Ekman Group, "Lie to Me," accessed February 8, 2016, www.paulekman.com/lie-to-me/.

[9]Robert L. Saucy, "Theology of Human Nature," in *Christian Perspectives on Being*

Human: A Multidisciplinary Approach to Integration, eds. J. P. Moreland and David M. Ciocchi (Grand Rapids, MI: Baker Books, 1993), 35.

[10]David Benner, *Care of Souls: Revisioning Christian Nurture and Counsel* (Grand Rapids, MI: Baker Books, 1998).

[11]This case material is adapted with permission from Todd W. Hall, "Psychoanalysis, Attachment, and Spirituality Part II: The Spiritual Stories We Live By," *Journal of Psychology and Theology* 35, no. 1 (March 2007): 29-42, https://doi.org/10.1177/009164710703500103.

5. ONCE MORE WITH FEELING

[1]Antonio Damasio, *The Feeling of What Happens* (San Diego: Harcourt, 1999).

[2]This section is adapted with permission from Todd Hall, "3 Practices to Harness the Power of Your Gut Level Knowledge," *Connection Culture Group* blog, October 18, 2015, www.connectionculture.com/post/3-practices-to-harness-the-power-of-your-gut-level-knowledge.

[3]Michael Heller and Véronique Haynal, "The Doctor's Face: A Mirror of His Patient's Suicidal Projects," in *The Body in Psychotherapy*, ed. J. Guimon (Basel, Switzerland: Karger, 1997), 46-51.

[4]Daniel Goleman, *Social Intelligence: The New Science of Human Relationships* (New York: Bantam Books, 2006), 15.

[5]Portions of this section adapted with permission from Todd Hall, "3 Ways Story Can Help You Create a Meaningful Life," *Dr. Todd Hall* blog, accessed March 14, 2022, www.drtoddhall.com/3-ways-story-can-help-you-create-a-meaningful-life/.

[6]Robert McKee, *Story: Substance, Structure, Style, and the Principles of Screenwriting* (New York: HarperCollins, 1997), 110.

[7]Robert McKee, *Story*.

[8]Robert McKee, *Story*, 111.

[9]Christopher Bollas, *The Shadow of the Object: Psychoanalysis of the Unthought Known* (New York: Columbia University Press, 1987).

[10]Antonio R. Damasio, *Descartes' Error: Emotion, Reason, and the Human Brain* (New York: Grosset/Putnam, 1994); Brent J. Atkinson, *Emotional Intelligence in Couples Therapy* (New York: Norton, 2005).

[11]Michael A. Rousell, *Sudden Influence: How Spontaneous Events Shape Our Lives* (Westport: Praeger, 2007), 70.

[12]Antonio Damasio, "When Emotions Make Better Decisions," FORA.tv, August 11, 2009, YouTube, www.youtube.com/watch?v=1wup_K2WN0I.

6. BORN TO CONNECT

[1]John Bowlby, "Forty-Four Juvenile Thieves: Their Characters and Home Life," *International Journal of Psychoanalysis* 25 (1944): 1-57.

[2]Portions of this section are adapted with permission from Todd W. Hall, "Psychoanalysis, Attachment, and Spirituality Part I: The Emergence of Two Relational Traditions," *Journal of Psychology and Theology* 35, no. 1 (March 2007): 14-28, https://doi.org/10.1177/009164710703500102.

[3]John Bowlby, *Maternal Care and Mental Health*, Monograph Series, no. 2 (Geneva: World Health Organization, 1951).

[4]John Bowlby, *Child Care and the Growth of Love* (London: Penguin Books, 1953; new and enlarged edition, 1965).

[5]James Robertson, *A Two-Year-Old Goes to Hospital* (London: Tavistock Child Development Research Unit; New York: University Film Library, 1952).

[6]Rene A. Spitz with Katherine M. Wolf, *Grief: A Peril in Infancy* (University Park, PA: PennState Media Sales, 1947).

[7]John Bowlby, "Separation Anxiety," *International Journal of Psycho-Analysis* 41 (1960): 89-113; and John Bowlby, *Separation: Anxiety and Anger*, 2nd ed. (New York: Basic Books, 1973), chapter 2.

[8]Quoted in Rene Spitz, "Hospitalism: An Inquiry Into the Genesis of Psychiatric Conditions in Early Childhood," *Psychoanalytic Study of the Child* 1 (1945): 53-74.

[9]Robert Karen, *Becoming Attached: First Relationships and How They Shape Our Capacity to Love* (New York: Oxford University Press, 1998).

[10]John Bowlby, *Attachment and Loss* (New York: Basic Books, 1982), 1: xxvii-xxviii.

[11]Paula R. Pietromonaco and Nancy L. Collins, "Interpersonal Mechanisms Linking Close Relationships to Health," *American Psychologist* 72 (2017): 531-42.

[12]Kane et al., "Comprehensive Versus Usual Community Care for First-Episode Psychosis: 2-Year Outcomes from the NIMH RAISE Early Treatment Program," *The American Journal of Psychiatry* 173, no. 4 (October 2015).

[13]Stephen J. Suomi, "Developmental Trajectories, Early Experiences, and Community Consequences," in *Developmental Health and the Wealth of Nations: Social Biological and Educational Dynamics*, eds. Daniel P. Keating and Clyde Hertzman (New York: Guilford Press, 1999), 189-200.

[14]Commission on Children at Risk, *Hardwired to Connect: The New Scientific Case for Authoritative Communities* (New York: Institute for American Values, 2003), 15.

[15]Daniel J. Siegel, *The Developing Mind*, 3rd ed. (New York: Guilford Press, 2020); and Commission on Children at Risk, *Hardwired to Connect*.

[16]Daniel J. Siegel, *The Developing Mind*. See also Michael J. Meaney, "Maternal Care, Gene Expression, and the Transmission of Individual Differences in Stress

Reactivity Across Generations," *Annual Review of Neuroscience* 24 (2001): 1161-92.
[17]Commission on Children at Risk, *Hardwired to Connect*, 55.

7. Becoming Attached

[1]Commission on Children at Risk, *Hardwired to Connect: The New Scientific Case for Authoritative Communities* (New York: Institute for American Values, 2003), 16.
[2]Commission on Children at Risk, *Hardwired to Connect*, 15.
[3]There are numerous lines of research going back to the 1950s that support the idea that people become attached to God. For example, people tend to describe God in relational terms; see Bernard Spilka, Philip Armatas, and June Nussbaum, "The Concept of God: A Factor-Analytic Approach," *Review of Religious Research* 6, no. 1 (1964): 28-36. People also tend to turn to God when they experience loss; see Ralph W. Hood, Peter C. Hill, and Bernie Spill, *The Psychology of Religion: An Empirical Approach*, 2nd ed. (New York: The Guilford Press, 2009); William James, *The Varieties of Religious Experience* (New York: Collier, 1902 and 1961). In addition, an in-depth interview study found that people both describe and experience God in ways that map well onto an attachment figure; see Marie-Therese Proctor, "The God Attachment Interview Schedule: Implicit and Explicit Assessment of Attachment to God" (PhD diss., University of Western Sydney, 2006).
[4]Justification refers to the idea that God does not credit our actual righteousness to our "account." Rather, when we put our trust in Christ, God credits Christ's righteousness to our account. Although we are still sinful in actuality, God declares us to be righteous and imputes Christ's righteousness to us. For extended discussions of this idea, see Romans 3:21-5:11 and Galatians 2:11-3:25.
[5]Hall et al., "Attachment to God and Implicit Spirituality: Clarifying Correspondence and Compensation Models," *Journal of Psychology and Theology* 37, no. 4 (2009): 227-42.
[6]A. Birgegard and P. Granqvist, "The Correspondence Between Attachment to Parents and God: Three Experiments Using Subliminal Separation Cues," *Personality and Social Psychology Bulletin* 30 (2004): 1122-35; Annie Fujikawa, Todd W. Hall, Steven L. Porter, and Christina Lee-Kim, "The Relationship Between Adult and God Attachment," (unpublished manuscript, Biola University, 2010); Todd W. Hall and Annie Fujikawa, "God Images and the Sacred" in *APA Handbook of Psychology, Religion, and Spirituality*, editor in chief Kenneth I. Pargament (Washington, DC: American Psychological Association, 2013), 277-92.

8. How We Connect to God and Others

[1]Jed Diamond, *The Irritable Male Syndrome: Managing the Four Key Causes of Depression and Aggression* (Emmaus, PA: Rodale, 2004); W. Rutz, et al., "Prevention of Male Suicides: Lessons from Gotland Study," *Lancet* 345 (1995): 524.

[2]Todd W. Hall with M. Elizabeth Lewis Hall, *Relational Spirituality: A Psychological-Theological Paradigm for Transformation* (Downers Grove, IL: IVP Academic, 2021).

[3]Jeffry A. Simpson, Williams S. Rholes, and Julia S. Nelligan, "Support Seeking and Support Giving Within Couples in an Anxiety-Provoking Situations: The Role of Attachment Styles," *Journal of Personality and Social Psychology* 62 (1992): 434-46.

[4]Portions of this section on secure attachment are adapted with permission from Todd W. Hall, "Psychoanalysis, Attachment, and Spirituality Part I: The Emergence of Two Relational Traditions," *Journal of Psychology and Theology* 35, no. 1 (March 2007): 14-28, https://doi.org/10.1177/009164710703500102.

[5]Hall et al., "Attachment to God and Implicit Spirituality: Clarifying Correspondence and Compensation Models," *Journal of Psychology and Theology* 37, no. 4 (2009): 227-42.

[6]E. Allison Peers, *The Dark Night of the Soul: A Masterpiece in the Literature by St. John of the Cross*, trans. and ed. E. Allison Peers (New York: Image Books, Doubleday, 1990).

[7]Marie-Therese Proctor, "The God Attachment Interview Schedule: Implicit and Explicit Assessment of Attachment to God" (PhD diss., University of Western Sydney, 2006).

[8]David J. Wallin, *Attachment in Psychotherapy* (New York: Guilford, 2007), chapter 13.

[9]Portions of this section on preoccupied attachment are adapted with permission from Hall, "Psychoanalysis, Attachment, and Spirituality Part I," 14-28.

[10]M. Mikulincer and I. Orbach, "Attachment Styles and Repressive Defensiveness: The Accessibility and Architecture of Affective Memories," *Journal of Personality and Social Psychology* 68 (1995): 917-25.

[11]M. Mikulincer and O. Nachshon, "Attachment Styles and Patterns of Self-Disclosure," *Journal of Personality and Social Psychology* 61, no. 2 (1991): 321-32.

[12]M. Mikulincer, "Adult Attachment Style and Information Processing: Individual Differences in Curiosity and Cognitive Closure," *Journal of Personality and Social Psychology* 72 (1997): 1217-30.

[13]M. Mikulincer, "Adult Attachment Style and Affect Regulation: Strategic Variations in Self-Appraisals," *Journal of Personality and Social Psychology* 75 (1998): 420-35, https://doi.org/10.1037/0022-3514.75.2.420.

[14]M. Mikulincer and D. Arad, "Attachment, Working Models, and Cognitive Openness in Close Relationships: A Test of Chronic and Temporary Accessibility Effects," *Journal of Personality and Social Psychology* 77 (1999): 710-25.

[15]Hall, et al., "Attachment to God and Implicit Spirituality," 227-42.

[16]Lee A. Kirkpatrick, "God as a Substitute Attachment Figure: A Longitudinal Study of Adult Attachment Style and Religious Change in College Students," *Personality and Social Psychology Bulletin* 24, no. 9 (1998): 961-73.

[17]K. R. Byrd and A. Boe, "The Correspondence Between Attachment Dimensions and Prayer in College Students," *The International Journal for the Psychology of Religion* 11, no. 1 (2001): 9-24.

[18]Proctor, "The God Attachment Interview Schedule."

[19]Wallin, *Attachment in Psychotherapy*, 217.

[20]P. R. Shaver and M. Mikulincer, "Attachment-Related Psychodynamics," *Attachment & Human Development* 4, no. 2 (2002): 133-61.

[21]Mikulincer and Orbach, "Attachment Styles and Repressive Defensiveness," 917-25.

[22]M. Mikulincer, "Adult Attachment Style and Individual Differences in Functional versus Dysfunctional Experiences of Anger," *Journal of Personality and Social Psychology* 74 (1998): 513-524.

[23]Mikulincer and Nachshon, "Attachment Styles and Patterns of Self-Disclosure," 321-32.

[24]J. A. Simpson, "Influence of Attachment Style on Romantic Relationships," *Journal of Personality and Social Psychology* 59, no. 5 (1990): 971-80.

[25]M. C. Pistole and F. Arricale, "Understanding Attachment: Beliefs About Conflict," *Journal of Counseling & Development* 81, no. 3 (2003): 318-28; J. C. Babcock et al., "Attachment, Emotional Regulation, and the Function of Marital Violence: Differences Between Security, Preoccupied, and Dismissing Violent and Nonviolent Husbands," *Journal of Family Violence* 15 (2000): 391-409.

[26]Portions of this section on dismissing attachment are adapted with permission from Hall, "Psychoanalysis, Attachment, and Spirituality Part I," 14-28.

[27]Hall et al., "Attachment to God and Implicit Spirituality," 227-42.

[28]Adapted with permission from Hall and Lewis Hall, *Relational Spirituality*, 166.

[29]Byrd and Boe, "The Correspondence Between Attachment Dimensions and Prayer," 9-24.

[30]Stephen A. Mitchell, "Object Relations Theories and the Developmental Tilt," *Contemporary Psychoanalysis* 20, no. 4 (1984): 1-19.

[31]Mary Main, "Metacognitive Knowledge, Metacognitive Monitoring, and Singular (coherent) vs. Multiple (incoherent) Models of Attachment: Findings and

Directions for Future Research," in *Attachment Across the Lifecycle*, ed. P. Harris, J. Stevenson-Hinde, and C. Parkes (New York: Routledge, 1991), 127-59.

[32]Daniel J. Siegel, *The Developing Mind*, 3rd ed. (New York: Guilford Press, 2020), 361.

[33]John Bowlby, *Attachment and Loss, Volume I: Attachment*, 2nd ed. (New York: Basic Books, 1982) xxvii-xxviii.

[34]*Cigna U.S. Loneliness Index: Survey of 20,000 Americans Examining Behaviors Driving Loneliness in the United States* (Cigna: Ipsos, 2018), accessed May 26, 2018, www.multivu.com/players/English/8294451-cigna-us-loneliness-survey/.

9. BORN TO LOVE

[1]Alexander Pruss, *One Body: An Essay in Christian Sexual Ethics* (Notre Dame, IN: Notre Dame Press, 2013), 23-27. These are drawn from Thomas Aquinas's theory of love; see Eleonore Stump, *Wandering in Darkness: Narrative and the Problem of Suffering* (Oxford: Oxford University Press, 2010), 91.

[2]Stephen G. Post, *Unlimited Love: Altruism, Compassion, and Service* (Philadelphia: Templeton Foundation Press, 2003).

[3]Jonathan T. Pennington and Charles H. Hackney, "Resourcing a Christian Positive Psychology from the Sermon on the Mount," *The Journal of Positive Psychology* 12, no. 5 (2017): 427-35, https://doi.org/10.1080/17439760.2016.1228008.

[4]C. S. Lewis, *The Four Loves* (New York: Harcourt, 1960), 49.

[5]Stump, *Wandering in Darkness*.

[6]Daniel Siegel, *The Developing Mind*, 3rd ed. (New York: Guilford Press, 2020), 170.

[7]Lewis, *The Four Loves*. Also see Todd W. Hall with M. Elizabeth Lewis Hall, *Relational Spirituality: A Psychological-Theological Framework for Spiritual Transformation* (Downers Grove, IL: IVP Academic, 2021).

[8]Stump, *Wandering in Darkness*, 97-100.

[9]Post, *Unlimited Love*, 5-6.

[10]"Every love has its art." Lewis, *The Four Loves*, 44. See also Lewis, *The Four Loves*, 55.

10. DEEP LOVE

[1]Pitirim A. Sorokin, *The Ways and Power of Love: Types, Factors, and Techniques of Moral Transformation* (Philadelphia: Templeton Foundation Press, 2002 [original 1954]), 16.

[2]Stephen G. Post, *Unlimited Love: Altruism, Compassion, and Service* (Philadelphia: Templeton Foundation Press, 2003), 32.

[3]This section is adapted with permission from Todd Hall, "3 Practices to Love Your Little Corner of the World, and Beyond," *Connection Culture Group* blog, October

3, 2015, www.connectionculture.com/post/3-practices-to-love-your-little-corner -of-the-world-and-beyond.

[4]Nicholas Wolterstorff, *Justice in Love* (Grand Rapids, MI: Eerdmans, 2015).

[5]Post, *Unlimited Love*, 108.

[6]Samuel P. Oliner and Pearl M. Oliner, *The Altruistic Personality: Rescuers of Jews in Nazi Europe* (New York: Free Press, 1988).

[7]Oliner and Oliner, *The Altruistic Personality*, 249.

[8]Oliner and Oliner, *The Altruistic Personality*, 186.

[9]Post, *Unlimited Love*, 127.

[10]Gerhard Lohfink, *Jesus and Community* (Philadelphia: Fortress Press, 1982).

[11]Post, *Unlimited Love*, 123.

[12]Garth A. Hallett, *Priorities and Christian Ethics* (Cambridge: Cambridge University Press, 1998).

[13]Post, *Unlimited Love*, 124.

[14]Lewis, *The Four Loves*, 116.

[15]Lewis, *The Four Loves*, 133.

[16]Lewis, *The Four Loves*, 128.

[17]Lewis, *The Four Loves*, 130.

[18]Lewis, *The Four Loves*, 130.

[19]Lewis, *The Four Loves*, 131.

[20]Stanley J. Grenz, *The Social God and the Relational Self: A Trinitarian Theology of the Imago Dei* (Louisville: Westminster John Knox Press, 2001), 313.

[21]William Plummer, "In a Supreme Act of Forgiveness, a Kentucky Couple 'Adopts' the Man Who Killed Their Son," *People*, August 26, 1985, https://people.com /archive/in-a-supreme-act-of-forgiveness-a-kentucky-couple-adopts-the-man -who-killed-their-son-vol-24-no-9/.

[22]Alexander Pruss, *One Body: An Essay in Christian Sexual Ethics* (Notre Dame, IN: Notre Dame Press, 2013), 18.

[23]Lewis, *The Four Loves*, 133.

11. UNDERSTANDING DEEP GROWTH

[1]Portions of this section are adapted with permission from Todd W. Hall with M. Elizabeth Lewis Hall, *Relational Spirituality: A Psychological-Theological Paradigm for Transformation* (Downers Grove, IL: IVP Academic, 2021), chapter 8.

[2]Allan Schore, *Affect Regulation and Disorders of the Self* (New York: W.W. Norton and Co., 2003), 89.

[3]Wilma Bucci, *Psychoanalysis and Cognitive Science* (New York: Guildford Press, 1997).

[4]Robert McKee, *Story: Substance, Structure, Style, and the Principles of Screenwriting* (New York: HarperCollins, 1997), 110.

[5]Christopher Bollas, *The Shadow of the Object: Psychoanalysis of the Unthought Known* (New York: Columbia University Press, 1987).

[6]This section is adapted with permission from Todd W. Hall, "Psychoanalysis, Attachment, and Spirituality Part II: The Spiritual Stories We Live By," *Journal of Psychology and Theology* 35, no. 1 (March 2007): 29-42, https://doi.org/10.1177/009164710703500103.

[7]Daniel J. Siegel, *The Developing Mind*, 3rd ed. (New York: Guilford Press, 2020), 150-55.

[8]This section is adapted with permission from Todd Hall, "3 Ways Story Can Help You Create a Meaningful Life," *Dr. Todd Hall* blog, accessed March 14, 2022, www.drtoddhall.com/3-ways-story-can-help-you-create-a-meaningful-life/.

[9]McKee, *Story*, 111.

[10]*Martian Child*, directed by Menno Meyjes (Los Angeles: New Line Cinema, 2007).

[11]McKee, *Story*, 110.

[12]Scott Duvall and J. Daniel Hays, *God's Relational Presence: The Cohesive Center of Biblical Theology*, (Grand Rapids, MI: Baker, 2019). As noted previously, Duvall and Hays argue that God's relational presence is the central theme of the entire biblical narrative.

12. CULTIVATING DEEP GROWTH

[1]J. K. Rowling, *Harry Potter and the Chamber of Secrets* (New York: Bloomsbury Children's Books), 333.

[2]Anders Ericsson and Robert Pool, *Peak: Secrets from the New Science of Expertise* (New York: Houghton Mifflin Harcourt, 2016).

[3]Dallas Willard, "Spiritual Disciplines, Spiritual Formation, and the Restoration of the Soul," *Journal of Psychology and Theology* 26 (1998): 106.

[4]Eric L. Johnson, "How God is Good for the Soul," *Journal of Psychology and Christianity* 22 (2003): 78-88.

[5]Jonathan T. Pennington and Charles H. Hackney, "Resourcing a Christian Positive Psychology from the Sermon on the Mount," *The Journal of Positive Psychology* 12, no. 5 (2017): 427-35, https://doi.org/10.1080/17439760.2016.1228008.

[6]N. T. Wright, *After You Believe: Why Christian Character Matters* (New York: HarperOne, 2010), 261.

[7]Todd W. Hall with M. Elizabeth Hall, *Relational Spirituality: A Psychological-Theological Paradigm for Transformation* (Downers Grove, IL: IVP Academic, 2021), chapter 1.

[8]Wright, *After You Believe*, 266.

[9]Stephen P. Stratton, "Mindfulness and Contemplation: Secular and Religious Traditions in Western Context," *Counseling and Values* 60 (2015): 100-118.

[10]Daniel J. Siegel, *The Mindful Brain: Reflection and Attunement in the Cultivation of Well-Being* (New York: W. W. Norton, 2007).

[11]Stratton, "Mindfulness and Contemplation," 109.

[12]Natasha Monroe and Peter J. Jankowski, "The Effectiveness of a Prayer Intervention in Promoting Change in Perceived Attachment to God, Positive Affect, and Psychological Distress," *Psychology of Religion & Spirituality* 3 (2016): 237-49.

[13]Stratton, "Mindfulness and Contemplation," 111.

[14]J. K. Ferguson, E. W. Willemsen, and M. V. Castañeto, "Centering Prayer as a Healing Response to Everyday Stress: A Psychological and Spiritual Process," *Pastoral Psychology* 59 (2010): 305-29.

[15]A. B. Wachholtz and K. I. Pargament, "Is Spirituality a Critical Ingredient of Meditation? Comparing the Effects of Spiritual Meditation, Secular Meditation, and Relaxation on Spiritual, Psychological, Cardiac, and Pain Outcomes," *Journal of Behavioral Medicine* 28 (2005): 369-84.

[16]Monroe and Jankowski, "The Effectiveness of a Prayer Intervention."

[17]Siegel, *The Mindful Brain*.

[18]C. A. Pepping, P. J. Davis, and A. O'Donovan, "Individual Differences in Attachment and Dispositional Mindfulness: The Mediating Role of Emotion Regulation," *Personality and Individual Differences* 54 (2013): 453-56; P. R. Shaver et al., "Social Foundations of the Capacity for Mindfulness: An Attachment Perspective," *Psychological Inquiry* 18 (2007): 264-71.

[19]R. M. Hertz, H. K. Laurent, and S. M. Laurent, "Attachment Mediates Effects of Trait Mindfulness on Stress Responses to Conflict," *Mindfulness* 6 (2015): 483-89; R. M. Ryan, K. W. Brown, and J. D. Creswell, "How Integrative is Attachment Theory? Unpacking the Meaning and Significance of Felt Security," *Psychological Inquiry* 18 (2007): 177-82.

[20]Hertz, Laurent, and Laurent, "Attachment Mediates Effects of Trait Mindfulness." See also Siegel, *The Mindful Brain*.

[21]Richard J. Davidson, "Well-Being and Affective Style: Neural Substrates and Biobehavioral Correlates," *Philosophical Transactions Royal Society London, Series B* 359 (2004): 1395-411.

[22]Adapted with permission from Hall with Lewis Hall, *Relational Spirituality*, 252-53.

13. SUFFERING WELL

[1]Portions of this chapter are adapted with permission from Todd W. Hall with M. Elizabeth Lewis Hall, *Relational Spirituality: A Psychological-Theological Paradigm for Transformation* (Downers Grove, IL: IVP Academic, 2021).

[2]D. Edmond Hiebert, "Selected Studies from 1 Peter Part 1: Following Christ's Example: An Exposition of 1 Peter 2:21-25," *Bibliotheca Sacra* 139, no. 553 (1982): 32-45.

[3]I am drawing here on M. Elizabeth Lewis Hall, "Suffering in God's Presence: The Role of Lament in Transformation," *Journal of Spiritual Formation & Soul Care* 9, no. 2 (2016): 219-32.

[4]Glenn Pemberton, *Hurting with God* (Abilene, TX: Abilene Christian University Press, 2012), 65.

[5]Richard G. Tedeschi and Lawrence G. Calhoun, *Trauma and Transformation: Growing in the Aftermath of Suffering* (Thousand Oaks: Sage, 1995), 1.

[6]Lawrence G. Calhoun and Richard G. Tedeschi, "The Foundations of Posttraumatic Growth: An Expanded Framework," in *Handbook of Posttraumatic Growth: Research and Practice*, eds. Lawrence G. Calhoun and Richard G. Tedeschi (Mahwah, NJ: Erlbaum, 2006), 3-23.

[7]Calhoun and Tedeschi, "The Foundations of Posttraumatic Growth," 3-23; Stephen Joseph and P. Alex Linley, "Growth Following Adversity: Theoretical Perspectives and Implications for Clinical Practice," *Clinical Psychology Review* 26 (January 2007): 1041-53.

[8]Joseph and Linley, "Growth Following Adversity," 1041-53.

[9]Christopher Petersen et al., "Strengths of Character and Posttraumatic Growth," *Journal of Traumatic Stress* 21, no. 2 (2008): 214-17.

[10]Calhoun and Tedeschi, "The Foundations of Posttraumatic Growth," 3-23; Joseph and Linley, "Growth Following Adversity," 1041-53.

[11]J. Irene Harris et al., "Coping Functions of Prayer and Posttraumatic Growth," *The International Journal for the Psychology of Religion* 20 (2010): 26-38.

14. BORN TO BELONG

[1]Chelsea Krueger, Todd W. Hall, and David Wang, "Spirituality in Transition: A Grounded Theory of Christians in Late Emerging Adulthood" (paper presented at the CAPS Annual Virtual Conference, March 2021).

[2]Gerhard Lohfink, *Jesus and Community* (Philadelphia: Fortress Press, 1984), 106.

[3]Kathleen Kovner Kline, ed., *Authoritative Communities: The Scientific Case for Nurturing the Whole Child* (New York: Springer, 2008), xiii-xiv.

[4]The Commission on Children at Risk, "Hardwired to Connect: The New Scientific Case for Authoritative Communities" in *Authoritative Communities: The*

Scientific Case for Nurturing the Whole Child, ed. Kathleen Kovner Kline (New York: Springer, 2008), 9.

[5]The Commission on Children at Risk, "Hardwired to Connect," 26.

[6]The Commission on Children at Risk, "Hardwired to Connect," 27.

[7]Byron R. Johnson, "A Tale of Two Religious Effects: Evidence for the Protective and Prosocial Impact of Organic Religion" in *Authoritative Communities: The Scientific Case for Nurturing the Whole Child*, ed. Kathleen Kovner Kline (New York: Springer, 2008), 187-225.

[8]Barbara M. Stilwell, "The Consolidation of Conscience in Adolescence" in *Authoritative Communities: The Scientific Case for Nurturing the Whole Child*, ed. Kathleen Kovner Kline (2008, New York: Springer), 123-50.

[9]Peter Block, *Community: The Structure of Belonging* (San Francisco: Berrett-Koehler, 2008).

[10]David Benner, *Presence and Encounter: The Sacramental Possibilities of Everyday Life* (Grand Rapids, MI: Brazos Press, 2014), 87.

[11]David Benner, *Presence and Encounter*, 88.